MARK DeVRIES AND NATE STRATMAN
AUTHOR OF *SUSTAINABLE YOUTH MINISTRY*

Name	Phone

BUILDING YOUR VOLUNTEER TEAM

A 30-DAY CHANGE PROJECT FOR YOUTH MINISTRY

IVP Books

An imprint of InterVarsity Press
Downers Grove, Illinois

InterVarsity Press
P.O. Box 1400, Downers Grove, IL 60515-1426
ivpress.com
email@ivpress.com

InterVarsity Press® is the book-publishing division of InterVarsity Christian Fellowship/USA®, a movement of students and faculty active on campus at hundreds of universities, colleges and schools of nursing in the United States of America, and a member movement of the International Fellowship of Evangelical Students. For information about local and regional activities, visit intervarsity.org.

All Scripture quotations, unless otherwise indicated, are taken from THE HOLY BIBLE, NEW INTERNATIONAL VERSION®, NIV® Copyright © 1973, 1978, 1984, 2011 by Biblica, Inc.™ Used by permission. All rights reserved worldwide.

While any stories in this book are true, some names and identifying information may have been changed to protect the privacy of individuals.

Cover design: David Fassett
Interior design: Beth McGill
Images: bird, star and face: © topform84/iStockphoto; clipboard: © RoscoPhoto/iStockphoto;
    clipboard: © Klosfoto/iStckphoto; name tags: © -1001-/iStockphoto;
    pen: © EnTock/iStockphoto; rock on a string: © ivstiv/iStockphoto

ISBN 978-0-8308-4121-9 (print)
ISBN 978-0-8308-9763-6 (digital)

Printed in the United States of America ∞

 As a member of the Green Press Initiative, InterVarsity Press is committed to protecting the environment and to the responsible use of natural resources. To learn more, visit greenpressinitiative.org.

Library of Congress Cataloging-in-Publication Data
DeVries, Mark.
  Building your volunteer team : a 30-day change project for youth ministry/Mark DeVries and Nate Stratman.
      pages cm
  Includes bibliographical references.
  ISBN 978-0-8308-4121-9 (pbk. : alk. paper)
  1. Church work with youth—Textbooks. I. Title.
  BV4447.D4493 2014
  259.23—dc23
                                                                                    2014033873

| P | 20 | 19 | 18 | 17 | 16 | 15 | 14 | 13 | 12 | 11 | 10 | 9 | 8 | 7 | 6 | 5 | 4 | 3 | 2 | 1 |
| Y | 31 | 30 | 29 | 28 | 27 | 26 | 25 | 24 | 23 | 22 | 21 | 20 | 19 | 18 | 17 | 16 | 15 |

From Mark:

To John Baird, the reluctant prophet who,
for decades, changed more lives than I can count,
one spicy Sunday morning at a time.

From Nate:

To "General" Dave Patton who at seventy-two
has reflected the love of Jesus to teenagers for
fifty years and shows no sign of letting up.

Contents

 **INTRODUCTION**

Why 30-Day Change?

If you want to go fast, go alone.
If you want to go far, go together.

AFRICAN PROVERB

We're making a huge assumption about you: You wouldn't be in the business you are in, and you wouldn't have even picked up this book, if you didn't care about change. You want to see change in your own life. You want your life and ministry to be different a year from now than they are today. We share that passion with you.

And after watching way too many of our friends wallow in the same habitual treadmill of molasses for far too many years, we decided to do something about it.

This 30-Day Change project is about giving you the step-by-step support you need to actually make one of the most important changes you want to see in your ministry. It's a thirty-day boot camp that allows you to focus on a single area of your ministry and make it radically different at the end of your thirty days.

Successfully completing this project, though, begins with a single admission: being stuck is a choice.

We'll say it again: *being stuck is a choice.*

We stay stuck because we fail to give the sustained attention to a problem that solving it requires. We flit from one crisis to another, never giving any of them the intense, costly focus required to make any difference. Most people choose to stay stuck in an unsatisfactory situation until the pain of the status quo becomes greater than the pain required to change. And for some, not even pain is enough motivation to make changes that will make things different a year from now than they are today. But we don't *have* to be in the same place a year from now that we are today.

Remember this, though: Most of the things we spend our time on actually change nothing. Most of our time is spent on maintaining our current trajectory, not changing it. Listen to how leadership guru Peter Drucker describes it:

> In a social situation a very small number of events—10 percent to 20 percent at most—account for 90 percent of all results, whereas the great majority of events account for 10 percent or less of the results.[1]

Did you catch what Drucker is saying? Eighty to ninety percent of our actions *don't change a thing*! The 30-Day Change process is designed to focus our attention on that elusive 10 percent or so, on the actions that will leverage us into a different place a year from now.

You've probably read somewhere that it takes a certain number of days to form a habit. Some say twenty-one, some say ninety, and there are all kinds of opinions in between. What we do know is that habits create change and creating a habit requires sustained investment day in and day out for several weeks. We picked thirty days—four rhythmic weeks, with a launch day and a wrap day on either end.

Throughout these thirty days, we'll be your accountability partners, your coaches. Champion coaches know that simply doing the right things does not create champions; doing the right things *habitually* does. We know for sure that focus and repetition create habits, whether it's about exercise or diet or scheduling. The same is true in ministry.

The beauty of this process is that giving sustained attention to the top area of need in your ministry *will* create change that will ripple far beyond that single area of focus. When you begin to achieve success that has been out of reach for you in one area of your ministry, the confidence gained can't help but seep into the rest of your life and ministry as well.

One of our favorite sayings is "Done is the engine of more." If you want to see change multiplied exponentially in your ministry, start by focusing on a single area, targeting one incremental accomplishment after another. Eventually your sustained investments *will* hit a tipping point and the incremental changes will begin to show exponential results.

In the next thirty days, you will be guided to *think* in new ways about your ministry. But more importantly, we'll be walking you through the actions you'll need to take to create the kind of deep, sustainable change you desire. We are absolutely convinced that if you will take these steps in the next thirty days, your ministry will be different at the end of the thirty days. In fact, we guarantee it.

How to Use This Book

Though we hope you'll be inspired and informed each day as you think in new ways about your ministry, this book is not to be read through like a devotional or an encyclopedia. You've read enough books that you marked up, that encouraged you, that gave you *ideas.*

This book is designed to be *used* like a recipe, a blueprint or an action plan. It only makes sense if you put it into practice. So if you bought it with the idea of reading it through in a night (which you could easily do) and checking off the accomplishment of (yet) another book read, you will have missed the point. This is a book that only makes sense as you do what it says.

Here's the qualifier: Though we certainly want you to take personal responsibility to implement this process, it is in no way designed for you to operate in isolation.

There will be hundreds (thousands?) of things to keep you from tending to the steps required to create fundamental change in your ministry. You'll have emails to check, you'll have phone calls to return, you'll have people drop by your office to talk for "just a second."

That's why we encourage you to invite two other people to come along with you in this journey. These two people will be your prayer and accountability partners for the month of this project. Once a week you'll meet with this pair. In addition to praying for you, they will provide counsel and accountability and hold up a mirror to your ministry (to help you see from angles you might otherwise miss).

You'll be looking for people whom you trust (you need to be able to hear them), who are willing to read this book with you (they need to be available) and who you are confident will speak the truth to you (they need to do more than just agree with everything you already think). Be unapologetic with your prayer partners about your hope that this process will not simply create change in your ministry, but in you as a leader as well.

It Might Go Without Saying

But we'll say it anyway.

Too often we "professionals" do ministry as practical atheists. We tip our hats to the Holy Spirit, but put more confidence in *our* plans than in the unexplainable work of God beneath and beyond our plans.

Knowing our own tendencies to do ministry apart from God's work in us, we have built into the rhythm of each week a deliberate day for prayer and spiritual reflection. On this day, you'll be invited into discerning God's work in the past week as well as opening yourself to any new directions the Spirit may be stirring in you for the coming week.

We are convinced that change comes most naturally to those who live rhythmically, particularly those who punctuate their weeks with a day that is wholly different from the others. The ancient practice of sabbath keeping can be radically contemporary in its impact, transforming our busy, aimless churning into profoundly strategic impact. Your reflection day will be your sabbath day each week. There is a great article on this topic posted on our website at ministryarchitects.com/30-day-change-resources.[2] (Similar resources can be found at Mark DeVries's blog, *The Sustainable Life*, at markdevriesblog.com.) *We encourage you to make time to read this article before you begin the project.*

Your ministry is where it is, at some level, because someone has chosen, whether deliberately or unintentionally, for it to be where it is. Maybe you chose. Maybe your predecessor did. The good news is that you can move from where you are to where you want to be. Here's how the process will work.

BUILDING YOUR VOLUNTEER TEAM: A WEEKLY RHYTHM

By selecting this 30-Day Change resource, you've made clear that you care deeply about building a ministry that doesn't just orbit around you (and would fall apart like a house of cards when you left). We're making the assumption that you've also picked up this book because you desperately want to transform your current volunteer situation into a team with the capacity to accomplish all that God is calling your ministry to do.

We've designed this 30-Day Change project in four rhythmic weeks, bracketed by reflection days at the beginning and the end of each week. Before beginning, you'll want to sync the days with the rhythm of your current ministry (for example, if you have a regular sabbath day you might want to schedule your day seven on your sabbath and sync the rest of the thirty days from there).

After your initial launch day, your weekly rhythm will look like this:

Day one each week will always be a *balcony day*. Don't be confused by the fact that the first weekly day one will happen on day two of the thirty days!

Your balcony day is not time off. It is probably the most important "time on" in your entire week. During balcony time you will set the course for your week, prepare for any scheduling landmines in the upcoming days and identify the "mission critical" tasks you must address to create the kind of change you truly desire. Your balcony days will help you start to think on your toes instead of reacting from back on your heels during these thirty days.

Days two through six will be when you *work the process*. On each of these days you will spend between one and two hours *building your volunteer team*. Each day, we'll give you a brief lesson followed by step-by-step instructions. Following this process will add up to extraordinary change at the end of the thirty days.

Day seven will always be a *reflection day/sabbath day*. On this day you'll prepare for your next meeting with your prayer partners, observing what God has stirred in you and in your ministry in the previous week. As you observe your progress toward building your volunteer team (as well as what remains to do), you will also discern what God may be bubbling up for you for the coming week. This reflection will clear the deck and set the stage for your balcony day the next day.

ONE WARNING BEFORE YOU BEGIN

This crash course *will* deliver results, but only if you work the process.

The 30-Day Change process is not a gradualist approach. If you want to accomplish the goal of getting your volunteer team in place in six months, there are ways for you to do that, but this is not one of them.

This book is only for folks who want (maybe *need*) to create change *fast*, in thirty days or less. So if you're looking for something that won't interrupt your normal schedule, this isn't the approach you're looking for. This is a boot camp for your ministry. It may require that, on some days, you get less sleep. It may require that you fall behind on some of your maintenance tasks (the 90 percent of tasks that keep you right where you are).

So, here's what we ask:

Do only one 30-Day Change project at a time.

Do no more than two 30-Day Change projects in a year.

Carve out two hours a day, six days a week to complete the 30-Day assignments. Most days may not take that long, but many certainly will. If you've carved out the time on the front end you'll have the margin you need when you need it.

Finally, confirm that your church has child protection and safe sanctuary policies in place. If not, lobby for that process to begin because you are going to rapidly expand the volunteer base at your church!

One more note: We (Nate and Mark) have written this book together, but throughout the days ahead we will speak in the singular "I" for ease and readability. Each of us has experienced everything we write about. No doubt you have also.

Enough said. Let's launch.

 **DAY 1**

Launch Day

Where there are no oxen, the manger is empty,
but from the strength of an ox come abundant harvests.

PROVERBS 14:4

The words poured out of her mouth before she could stop them: "It's just easier for me to do it myself."

At one level, of course, this youth leader is right. Almost always it *is* easier to do it ourselves. We avoid the hassle of having to coordinate and communicate. We avoid having to follow up with people who drop the ball.

"Everyone is busy," we say to ourselves, "and *I'm* the one being paid for this work, right?"

We've heard dozens of reasons why leaders, even very intelligent and very spiritual ones, choose not to build a solid volunteer team. But quite frankly, the reasons are all rubbish.

Ministry is not singles tennis. It's more like football or hockey or baseball. It's the team that wins. Too many youth workers I know are like a coach who decides to save time on the front end by playing all the positions—quarterback, receiver, safety, linebacker. "It would be so much easier," I can imagine the coach saying, "if I didn't have to spend all that time recruiting! Think of all the time I would save in the off-season!" Coaches who didn't have to recruit would be free to focus on developing their own skills rather than going through the tedium of building a team.

I hope you're getting the absurd metaphor.

If you want to save time in the short run, you've got the wrong book. Faithful ministry is almost never meant to be a do-it-yourself project. It's a do-it-together project. You want a job you can do by yourself? Get a newspaper route. Be a telemarketer. Sell shoes. But ministry will require you to be a team builder more than a solo player. Of course, you know this already. It's why you picked up this book.

TODAY'S MISSION

1. Scan through the entire thirty-day plan (this book) to get a sense of the rhythms of the weeks.

2. Answer this question in writing, and be prepared to share your response with your prayer partners when you meet with them: *At the end of this 30-Day Change, how would I like my ministry to be different?* (Hints: How many volunteers? What kinds of volunteers? What's different about the recruiting process? The training process? How does it feel different?) You might know you've got this right when you read it and it creates a little lump in your throat.

3. Invite two people to be your prayer partners through this process—to pray for you and for the process, to meet with you weekly and to help you think through the implementation steps found in the next twenty-nine days. Suggest meeting times, ideally in a rhythm that lines up with your reflection days (days 8, 15, 22, 29).

4. Send an email or text or make a call to at least three previous volunteers who have left the youth ministry (or maybe even the church) in the last year or two. Let them know a little about this project, and invite them to give you some feedback to help you understand each of their particular reasons for no longer working as a volunteer. See the end of this chapter for a sample email you could send, including a few key questions to ask.

5. Determine what day you will carve out as your reflection day (or sabbath day) each week. On reflection days the assignments will take much less time. We have provided questions for you to work through in preparation for your weekly check-in with your prayer partners. Once you have determined when your reflection day will be each week, orient your thirty-day project around those days. For example, if you determine your reflection days will be on Thursdays, select a Thursday at least eight days away and make that day eight of this project. Make the day before day seven, and the day after day nine. Keep numbering days accordingly until all thirty have been assigned to a specific day on the calendar.

6. For each of the non-reflection days, schedule two hours to focus on your 30-Day Change project. It may not take two hours every day, but having the time set aside will ensure that you have appropriate margin to accomplish each 30-Day Change daily mission.

7. Read the following brief excerpt on recruitment from Mark's book *Sustainable Youth Ministry*.

RECRUITMENT: THE FIRST STEP IS THE HARDEST

The study behind the book *Youth Ministry That Transforms*[1] revealed that less than a third of professional youth workers experience regular success in recruiting volunteers. Less than a third! Our experience with youth workers bears this statistic out.

Quite accidentally, we stumbled onto the biggest obstacle in recruiting volunteer leaders. After working with church after church that just couldn't seem to get traction in recruiting volunteers, we started asking youth workers, "How many hours have you spent in the previous week actually recruiting volunteers?" Almost invariably, it was less than an hour (most often, it was exactly zero).

To get a youth worker off the dime, we recommend that he or she make five recruiting calls in the coming week. Since at this point we're not expecting a definite yes or no, we call these "cultivating calls" rather than recruiting calls. The assignment is not to recruit, but simply to make the first call (even if that is simply leaving a message). This process can take anywhere from ten to thirty minutes.

Before we end our conversation with the youth worker, we agree on the names of people he or she will call for what volunteer positions and agree to an accountability check the next week.

But when we check in a week later, the youth worker who "desperately" wants more volunteers has often not made a single call. *Something* has come up—an unusually busy ministry month, a student in crisis, a dog who ate the list.

We're talking about an assignment that could have been completed in less than thirty minutes, maybe in as little as ten. But the average youth worker has extraordinary difficulty finding those ten minutes.

Here's why: Recruiting is hard.

Few of us like to ask people to do things for us. Most of us would rather just do it ourselves than go through the discomfort of making calls. As a result, many youth workers step into the fall (when the season opens) unable to field a complete team and complaining about being overwhelmed.

This pattern perpetuates the myth that "no one in our church ever volunteers." Frantically cobbling together a group of volunteers who fill slots every other week or so reinforces the perception that they're only helpers in someone else's ministry. When we see a youth ministry with rotating helpers, we can be sure that there is dry rot in the foundation.

Sadly, most volunteer recruitment comes in the form of blanket solicitations to large groups. The assumption, of course, is that such an approach will save the recruiter time. But in the long run, blanket appeals always wind up taking *more* time, for very obvious reasons:

- Blanket appeals often attract volunteers who would simply not be appropriate to work with teenagers (I refer to blanket bulletin appeals as "pedophile invitations"). Getting the wrong person to stop being involved takes a lot more time than never having him or her involved in the first place.

- The kind of initiative-taking leaders we're looking for seldom flock to blanket announcements. They need to be recruited personally, one at a time. They'll need to be contacted anyway, so blanket appeals only multiply the amount of time required.

- A flurry of public announcements about the *desperate need* in the youth ministry perpetuates a climate of desperation, which almost always results in a flurry of unsolicited advice-giving from well-meaning church members and senior pastors who assume they need to help the youth worker fix his or her problem.

But hidden beneath all the reasons that recruiting doesn't work, there's good news: when those responsible for a youth ministry actually invest the appropriate amount of time in the recruitment process, at the right time, we can almost guarantee success.

We've seen lots of variations, shortcuts and "brilliant" ideas for recruiting volunteers (for example, some suggest that you have the kids recruit for you, or threaten to cancel a program if you don't have enough volunteers), but none of those work nearly as well as *working* a very clear process. Remember, we're investing, not gambling on great ideas.[2]

Sample email to previous volunteers

Dear [NAME],

I'm writing to ask a little favor.

You are someone I trust and respect, and I would really value your input on a project I am stepping into.

I'm working on building our volunteer team for our youth ministry for next year. As someone who has been but is not currently a youth leader, you have a perspective that can be incredibly helpful as I step into this season of building our team.

Would you be willing to answer a few questions for me? I've included them below. You can send me an email, or just call my voicemail (555-555-5555) and leave me your responses. I'm not looking for a well-prepared essay, just your immediate thoughts.

Thanks so much for the investment you've already made in our ministry. I look forward to hearing your thoughts and even more to the ways that your input will affect the way we build our next volunteer team.

Here are the questions:

- What were the biggest motivating factors in your choosing to serve in the youth ministry?

- What were the biggest motivating factors in your choosing to stop serving in the youth ministry?

- What was the most helpful thing the leadership of the youth ministry did to help you have a meaningful, impactful experience working with youth?

- What might the leadership of the youth ministry have done differently to have made your experience working with our youth more meaningful, more impactful or maybe even less of a hassle for you?

- If the leadership of the youth ministry had done the things you recommended in the previous question, might you still be serving in the youth ministry now?

Thanks so much for taking a little time to help us think through these questions together. Your input will be invaluable for us.

Blessings,
[NAME]

 **DAY 2**

Balcony Day

A View from Above

I must slow down, so I may make haste
in arriving at my destination.

ANONYMOUS HIGH SCHOOL ENGLISH TEACHER

We call it living rhythmically. It's fundamental to the way we have been designed. We were all made to live with a weekly rhythm.

In running it's called interval training, a regimen involving bursts of intensity followed by slowing down enough to let your heart rate return to a resting rate. It's widely accepted that adding interval workouts to a training plan naturally increases both endurance and speed.

Too many youth workers are exhausted, not because of the number of hours they work but because there are few, if any, parts of their normal week that are in any way different from the others. In short, there's no rhythm to their lives.

The combination of practicing a weekly sabbath and taking at least two hours of balcony time each week has a way of punctuating our weeks, refocusing our time *every week* on the things that matter most.

Balcony time is not time off. It is your most important time *on.* We want you to build balcony time into every week, not just during these thirty days but for the rest of your life. This is the day when you work *on* your life and ministry, not just in it. Balcony time is not your sabbath time, but it is the time when you make sure the rhythm of sabbath is built into your coming week. It's not devotional time, but it is the time when you make sure you are moving deliberately into the presence of God each week. It's not your exercise time, but it is the time when you recalibrate your schedule to maximize your physical health.

Without balcony time, our lives and ministries become increasingly cluttered with layers and layers of secondary priorities. We forget the things that make our hearts sing and fall into deepening ruts of sameness that keep us stuck on the gerbil wheel going nowhere, no matter how fast we run.

People who practice balcony time simply live with greater clarity, greater balance, greater stamina and greater joy in ministry. And they get a heck of a lot more done as well.

Here's why: like the narrowing of the walls of a river, balcony time creates a more powerful current. Because balcony time forces us to be deliberate about putting first things first, it limits the amount of time we have for time-sucking, meandering tasks like checking email dozens of times a day. Focusing first on our most important priorities leaves less time for everything else, naturally increasing our velocity and focus. Anyone who has gotten a week's worth of work done in a single day just before leaving for vacation knows exactly what we're talking about.

In balcony time there is no separation between personal and professional—it's your one chance a week to give focus, rhythm and passion to the *one* life you've been given to steward. During these thirty days we'll be setting the structure for your balcony time, in hopes that after four directed balcony times you'll be hooked for life.

Nothing will help you increase your capacity for change as much as balcony time and living rhythmically. If you would like to know more, grab a copy of Mark's book *Sustainable Youth Ministry* and check out chapters eight, "Aligning the Heart," and nine, "Monkeys, Frogs, and Balconies."

Now let's dive into your first balcony day.

TODAY'S MISSION

1. Begin to compile your 30-Day Change resource pile (or notebook, if you happen to experience pile aversion). By the end of your first week you will have added several other items to this pile, but on this day include

   o your church directory, ideally a pictorial one but definitely one with easily accessible contact information, including email addresses

   o a list of current volunteer leaders with their contact information

   o a list of all previous volunteer leaders from the past five to ten years, if possible

2. Create a photo wall of all your current volunteer leaders, to be used when you meet with your prayer partners on your sabbath day to pray for each leader by name. Each time a new leader is added to your team, include his or her picture on the prayer wall.

3. Take a quick inventory of your current volunteer leaders by answering these questions:

   o Which of my current volunteer leaders is exactly in the right role—not overwhelmed or under-challenged?

- Is there anyone on the team who would be delighted to do more if asked?

- Is there anyone on the team desperately in need of a break?

- Which leader is in the "wrong seat on the bus"—a role that doesn't fit well?

4. Lock in your weekly meeting times with your prayer partners for the next month.

5. Create a list of the top five challenges to having the kind of volunteer team you have wanted in your ministry.

 **DAY 3**

Partners Versus Helpers

Never try to teach a pig to sing.
It wastes your time and it annoys the pig.

PAUL DICKSON

Most youth ministers we've observed use a volunteer-development model we call "The Genius and A Hundred Helpers." Here's how it works: volunteers are recruited to *help* the youth minister do his or her job. It's understood that real ministry is what the youth minister does. Everyone else just "helps out." The favorite line of the helper is "Just call me if you need me." Many youth workers assume that if they could just get more helpers in their ministries, they could get so much more done, be less tired and minister more effectively.

The big problem with this approach is that every helper is waiting for *us* to take the initiative. A helper says, for example, "I'd love to help out in Sunday school on an as-needed basis. Just let me know the week before if you need me." So *every week* it is our responsibility to determine whether we need this helper. Then we have to call them *every time we need them* (usually requiring several attempts for each point of need). If the helper says yes, then we're responsible to get the curriculum to them, as well as all the needed supplies and attendance sheets.

No wonder so many people say, "It's just easier to do it myself." If they work with the "genius and a hundred helpers" model, trying to delegate and coordinate the small tasks of dozens of helpers, they'd be absolutely right. It could be, in fact, that the *last* thing a youth pastor needs is more helpers.

We like a different model. We call it the "Ministry Partner" model. In this model, a partner volunteer *owns* a piece of the ministry. The partner, for example, might *own* the youth Sunday school class. She ensures that curriculum is in place, that attendance is taken, that the room is set up, that inactive youth are followed up with and that substitutes are found when needed. The partner volunteer knows more about her ministry setting (and often the youth in it) than the staff person does. The partner is not waiting week after week for instructions from the "genius" youth pastor. The partner knows his or her mission and manages it, and the staff person *helps the partner* succeed.

Building your volunteer team starts with understanding the available partner roles in your ministry. Here are a few possibilities to prompt your thinking:

- Sunday school teachers who serve on autopilot week in and week out
- small group leaders
- major event coordinators
- youth group food coordinator
- weekly youth group leaders
- games coordinator

- youth music coordinator

- youth website and social media czar

- first-timer follow-up coordinator

- MIA youth follow-up coordinator

- trip and registration coordinator

- chair of the youth committee

Certainly, not all of these partner roles will apply in your setting, and there's a good chance you'll have a few more in your context that didn't make our list. The key is to start by identifying all the partner roles that are needed in your ministry. Don't worry at this point whether you've got the people in your church to fill those roles; just identify the roles.

Of course, you will have many helpers in your ministry—those who can drive or bring food or host an event. But if you are to best utilize the willingness of those helpers, you need partners who can coordinate their work, encourage them and celebrate with them. Today we start the process of locking in our partners *first*.

TODAY'S MISSION

1. Develop your needs list for partner volunteers. You can use the 30-Day Change Master Needs List Template in Word or Excel found at ministryarchitects.com/30-day-change-resources or make your own list on paper based on what you see there. You will include all the partner roles you will need for the coming year in your ministry.

2. Once you have completed the list of all your needed partner volunteers, count how many slots there are on your partner needs list. We're looking here for the total number of people you will need, not the number of different roles. So if you need six Sunday school teachers in one setting, that counts as six, not one.

3. Multiply the number of needed partner volunteers (from step 2) by three. For example, if you need twenty-five partner volunteers you multiply twenty-five by three and get seventy-five. (We're really not trying to make this feel like your 1040 tax form!)

4. Follow up with any of the three previous volunteers you haven't heard from to gather their input as you begin this project (see day 1, step 4).

 DAY 4

The Trap of Terminal Vagueness

Inspiration is the windfall from hard work and focus.
Muses are too unreliable to keep on the payroll.

HELEN HANSON

Most youth ministries live in the fuzzy ether of terminal vagueness. Some ministry leaders feel queasy about setting definite targets. It feels too much like a business. But of course, the alternative to having clear targets is having fuzzy ones. So we flounder, often directionless, letting the screaming priorities of everyone else set the course for our work. Like sailors navigating by the current and not by the stars, we find ourselves repeatedly crashing on the rocks, wondering how in the world we ever got there.

When we don't know what we want or what we need, we end up doing nothing to get there. We quickly embrace victim mentality, complaining that people *in our church* just aren't committed. There are few areas where this pattern is more common than in the world of recruiting volunteers.

But there's good news.

There is no magic formula for recruiting volunteers, no secret sauce that some lucky youth workers know. But there is a process. A process that almost always works. Building a solid volunteer team is as simple (and as hard) as this: *Invest time in working the process toward a very clear target, and you'll have all the volunteers you need.*

Very few of us actually *like* to pick up the phone and ask for something. But being a leader means, well, that we actually have a team to lead. A shocking number of youth workers step into their positions absolutely astonished that there is no team in place for them to lead, and they blame the church, the previous youth director or apathetic parents. As leaders, it's our job to build the team, and the first step in that process is to identify our needs. How many Sunday school teachers do we need? How many small group leaders? How many youth group leaders? How many major event coordinators?

Yesterday we developed your needs list. Today you take the next step: developing your "pool," or potential leader list.

Today's Mission

1. Review the partner needs list you developed yesterday using the 30-Day Change Master Needs Template. See if there are any positions you need to add or if you want to change the number of leaders needed for any given category, and update the list accordingly.

2. Create a potential volunteer pool list with the same number of blanks as the number you ended up with in step three from yesterday (for example, 75). Come up with names of everyone you can think of in your church who might be a potential volunteer. At this point you are not filtering or excluding any names, just including the names of anyone you think might have potential, whether you think they will say yes or not. At

this stage do not be concerned about whether they are already serving elsewhere in the church. Here are a couple of places to look for your potential volunteers:

- ○ Look through your church's directory for people who might volunteer.

- ○ Since it's likely that you don't know everyone in your church, reach out to ten or so folks who can serve as sources for you. We've actually included in the next section a sample email for you to send to your sources to give you a starting point. You'll want to keep asking until you come up with as many names as your targeted potential volunteer number. Send an email to

  - • your colleagues on staff

  - • well-networked parents

  - • student leaders

  - • current volunteer leaders

  - • church leadership—elders, deacons, adult Sunday school teachers

  - • saints and pillars of your church

3. Send an email or text to confirm your upcoming meeting with your prayer partners.

Sample email to sources

Hi [NAME],

It's [NAME] from church. I wonder if I could ask a quick favor.

I'm beginning the process of putting my team together to work with our youth ministry next year. I want to do everything I can to make sure we don't miss someone in our church who might be a great fit but whom I may not have gotten to know yet.

Could you float me a few names of folks you know in our church who you think might have gifts for working with our teenagers? These could be older adults, young adults, parents, college students—anyone you think may be a possibility. (You can even add yourself to that list if you might be feeling called to serve in the youth ministry, but this letter is not a backdoor attempt to ask you to serve!)

I'll personally follow up with every person you suggest to see if they might be a fit and to explain in more detail what we're looking for.

I'd be very grateful for any names you send my way (and if you happen to have their contact information, all the better).

Blessings,
[NAME]

 **DAY 5**

Progress, Not Perfection

I remember reading that Shakers deliberately introduced
a mistake into the things they made, to show that
man shouldn't aspire to the perfection of God.
Flawed can be more perfect than perfection.

GRETCHEN RUBIN, *THE HAPPINESS PROJECT*

One of the great impediments to building a healthy volunteer team is the unrealistic desire to get a perfect team together in the perfect way—immediately. Of course, we don't actually use the word *perfect*. Instead we talk about "finding the right fit." We talk about "not just filling slots!" We talk about waiting until the right time to ask.

I've seen youth pastors totally stymied in their recruiting process by the trap of perfectionism.

- There's the youth pastor who feels that every potential volunteer should have completed a spiritual gifts test (or a DISC profile or an Enneagram assessment or a Myers-Briggs survey or a strengths-finder report, or all of the above!).

- There's the youth leader who thinks no one should be qualified to lead until they have had at least twenty hours of training.

- There's the student ministries director at the Blue Hair Memorial Church who believes that only young adults should be youth leaders, and the youth worker at Skinny Jeans Community Church who believes that young adults are too inexperienced to provide real leadership to students.

I'm a fan of spiritual gifts tests. I'm a fan of youth volunteers being trained. I'm a fan of having older adults as youth leaders and having younger adults as youth leaders. These are great priorities, but again and again we've seen wonderful teams built without attention to these priorities!

Generally, focusing on getting all the right volunteer systems in place *before* you build your team almost always results in having little or no team to train. The trap of perfectionism keeps us paralyzed because we know all the things we'd *like* to do to build a great team of volunteers. Like starting up a hill with a bike in high gear, expecting the perfect recruiting or training processes has a way of stalling the momentum you'll need to build your team.

The first step of getting a team in place is (dare I say it?) filling the slots, making sure all the positions are filled for the coming year. Yes, we want to get the best possible people in the best possible roles. And the next twenty-four days we'll be focusing on just that priority.

This year, you will undoubtedly come up with things you'd like to do differently next year. When you do, write them down in a document called "Improving Our Recruiting Process." *But this year*, let's focus on building a gloriously imperfect team—the only kind of team God ever gets to work with.

TODAY'S MISSION

1. Create a document called "Improving Our Recruiting Process" (either on your computer or in a physical file). As you come across things you'd like to do differently when you start the recruiting process a year from now, include those ideas in this document.

2. On your potential pool list, write to the left side of each name one of the following letters:

   A—This person would be a *great* addition to your team.

   B—This person would be a good addition to your team.

   C—This person is a possible addition to your team.

3. To the right side of the names on your list, identify each person with one of the following letters:

   W—This person would be great working *with* kids.

   B—This person would be great working *behind* the scenes.

   E—This person would be great working in *either* kind of role—with kids or behind the scenes.

4. Place each name from your pool list into your master needs list (samples at ministryarchitects.com/30-day-change-resources) so that every blank has a single name in it. Each name should only be used once. You'll want to place the A names first, placing Ws and Es in roles working directly with students and Bs and Es in behind-the-scenes roles.

5. On your master needs list, include a phone number and email address for every name you have placed in a slot.

 **DAY 6**

Focusing on Next Year Before This Year

Someone's sitting in the shade today because
someone planted a tree a long time ago.

WARREN BUFFETT

I know it sounds crazy. But I'm suggesting that, when it comes to recruiting your volunteer team, you focus as much or more on next year's team as you do on this year's team.

Here's why:

1. Yes, you need to stop the bleeding around the urgent needs of this week. But tending to those needs *first* will only perpetuate the stuckness.

2. Your best potential, high-leverage, load-bearing volunteers are not likely available for the urgent needs you have this week. Because your best volunteers are natural leaders, they have organized their major commitments months, sometimes even years, in advance. You never get the greatest volunteers when you ask at the last minute.

3. The earlier you ask, the more likely you are to get a yes. I sometimes say that the difficulty of recruiting next fall's volunteers *doubles* each month after March, if this is your initial ask.

4. The earlier you ask, the more value your new volunteer will place on the position. I'm pretty certain that the PTA at the school across town already knows right now who its *next* president will be. Knowing your commitment six months or so in advance simply puts this new responsibility higher on your list.

So here's the challenge: before you deal with the crisis de jour with your current ministry this week, spend time *first* working to build a full team of leaders for the coming year. In a normal setting, we recommend starting the recruiting process of major, load-bearing, partner volunteers six months before they are to begin serving.

TODAY'S MISSION

Now that you've matched your pool list with your needs list, now that every blank is filled, it's time to get a single ask out to every person on your master needs list (we also call this your master recruiting list now that it has names in the blanks).

Send a personal email (like the one on the next page) to each person on your master list.

Hey [NAME],

I hope all is well in your world.

I've got a quick question for you, one that I realize may not have a quick answer!

I'm putting my team together for next year's _____ [for example, seventh grade Sunday school, small group program], and I would love for you [or you and spouse—using his or her name] to consider being a part of this team.

You may know right now that you can't take on another thing next year, starting [DATE]. If so, just give me a quick "call me another year" message, and I'll get back to you in six months or so. If you're a "maybe," let me know and I can give you a little more detail about what we're looking for and give you the chance to ask any questions you might have.

There are a handful of folks in the church who get to work with our teenagers, and I'd love for you to be one of them next year!

I look forward to hearing from you.

 **DAY 7**

Getting a Rhythm

> *We are what we repeatedly do.*
> *Excellence, then, is not an act, but a habit.*
>
> ARISTOTLE

Maybe you've heard of the "Write a Novel in Thirty Days" challenge. We have friends who have actually done it. Maybe you've watched *The Biggest Loser* and observed the way that 100 percent of the contestants on that show lose weight. It happens every time. In each case, someone made a decision to do something differently and turned that decision into a habit they focus on daily.

You have decided that during this thirty-day challenge you will make a habit, a *daily* time priority, of tending to the building of your volunteer team. Whether it's weight loss or writing or recruiting the best-ever volunteer team for a ministry, those who accomplish major change have two things in common: focus and persistence (coupled, of course, with the trump card of grace). Want to run a marathon? The formula is simple (not easy): time and persistence. Want your marriage to be better a year from now than it is today? Time and persistence. In *Blink*, Malcolm Gladwell reminds us that it takes ten thousand hours to become an expert at something, whether it is our jobs, our parenting, our money management or our favorite sport. As you finish up the first week of your thirty-day focus on building a volunteer team, you've likely found more than a few reasons not to find time for working on building your team.

At one level, accomplishing this mission is simply about applying the right pressure consistently, about building time into the rhythm of your day. The reason we've made a priority of weekly "balcony time" in this process is that taking that time forces us to face the fact that nothing is likely to change in our ministries without a change first happening in us.

Let me be offensively candid: you don't have the volunteer team in place that you would like because, well, because of you. This is not a statement of blame. It is actually a statement about the power you have to make things different.

Maybe you don't have the volunteer team you'd like in place because you have never learned how to recruit a team. Maybe it's because you've never learned how to recruit a team in a church context like your current one. Maybe there's some other reason. But when you take time to work *on* your ministry, not just *in* it, you accept responsibility to try (and fail) and try (and fail) until you discover the alchemy that has been missing from your approach to building a volunteer team.

Today's Mission

Today you'll begin the rhythmic work that you'll do most days throughout the rest of the 30-Day Change process.

1. Take out your master recruiting documents: your needs list and your ranked pool list.

2. Check your email to see if anyone has responded to your email invitation, and respond to those emails immediately.

3. For those who have said yes, send an email suggesting a meeting time and place for you to talk further about what you're looking for.

4. For those who have said no,

   ○ Move their names to the bottom of the pool list, under a new section called "No."

   ○ Beside each name, write what role each person has said no to.

   ○ Remove their names from the needs list.

5. Place new names in the blanks left by those who have said no.

6. Send your standard invitation email to the people you have just added to your master recruiting list.

 **DAY 8**

Reflection Day

Catch Your Breath

Six days you shall labor and do all your work,
but the seventh day is a sabbath to the LORD your God.

EXODUS 20:9-10

Well, how did you do this week?

If you're like us, you may have started out this first week with a passion; you may have jumped right in to the first couple of days with enthusiasm. And then, by day three or four, "life" started happening to you. Maybe your child got sick, or you had a big event to prepare for, or an unhappy parent rented all the extra space you may have had on your schedule or in your brain this week. It just doesn't take long for normal life and ministry (read: chaos) to wipe out any hope of progress, of structure, of order, does it?

Here's the good news: today is the day you take a breather from your 30-Day Change project. Hopefully, you've already scheduled your next meeting with your prayer partners and won't be meeting with them today, in order to give you a total break from this project. This is your sabbath day.

Feel free to reflect on and pray through the questions under Today's Mission below, or simply wait to talk them through with your prayer partners when you meet in a few days.

Regardless, catch your breath, and rest in the certainty that God is at work when we are not.

TODAY'S MISSION

1. When you meet with your prayer partners, share with them your answers to these questions:

   o What are you most excited about after having worked this process for a week?

   o What has been your biggest point of discouragement?

   o As you look at the next week, what times have you set aside to focus on the assignments you've been given?

   o How can your prayer partners be praying for you this week—whether about this thirty-day process or about anything else that you're experiencing as particularly pressing at this point in your life?

2. Share with your prayer partners the master recruiting documents you've developed and have started to use this week.

3. Pray together over the names of the folks you will particularly be focusing on this week and about any challenges you are facing in this process.

DAY 9

Balcony Day

Admitting the Existence of Normal

*Everybody has a plan until
they get punched in the face.*

MIKE TYSON

I don't know about you, but I'm often thrown off track by normal—by things I could have anticipated if I had looked into the details of my week before I started it. Things such as

- an all-day staff meeting
- a funeral *and* a wedding
- in-laws in town
- my daughter's dance recital

The truth is that most weeks we anticipate a predictable, calm "normal." In ministry, though (and in most "normal" lives), chaos, interruptions and the *un*predictable are the real normal. After doing lots of weekly coaching with youth pastors, I have come to expect most clients to describe their past and current weeks as "abnormal."

They say things like,

- "We had this retreat last weekend and . . ."
- "The baby was up almost all night the last three nights with the flu . . ."
- "We've got this big, annual campaign going on at church with tons of extra meetings."

Yes, these things are peculiar. But having something peculiar is all part of a *normal* week. So let's admit the existence of normal crazy weeks, but let's take time to prepare for navigating the inevitable chaos we'll be sailing through.

How? Today is your balcony day. Today you will take a couple of hours to work *on* your ministry. Today you move into the stance of being prepared for whatever is coming, while at the same time *keeping on track with your most important priorities.*

TODAY'S MISSION

1. Make the decision to give up the illusion that there will ever be a time in your life when you just naturally and regularly get everything on your daily task list done.

2. Make a master list of all those who have said yes to specific roles. Print out that list, including the role that each person has agreed to, and display it prominently in your office.

3. Take a look at your task list for the week (or create one, if this is not a natural part of the rhythm of your life yet). Identify your top priorities for the week. You are looking here for things that will make your life and ministry more the way you'd like them to be a year from now (not the screaming, urgent demands on your time). Your top priorities might include

- deliberate time with your family,

- time for specific spiritual disciplines

- and (of course) during these thirty days, two hours daily focused on building your volunteer team.

4. Complete your calendar for the week, including all currently scheduled appointments (such as meetings, programs and any other commitments). Now make appointments with yourself for the top priorities you identified in step two.

5. You may very well find that when you add your currently scheduled commitments and your top priorities, you are already out of time for the week (and you still have a few urgent things you've got to get to, not to mention returning emails and responding to voicemail). On some weeks this is *normal.* If this is the case for you this week, you've got some problem solving to do. Here's a start:

   - Corral your emails and phone calls into a specific time block for each day. If your week is packed, you simply don't have time to be immediately available this week. Plan on taking a break from Facebook and Twitter as well.

   - Determine what you will need to cut from your schedule, being careful not to cut any of your top priorities (those things that have the potential to make your life and ministry different a year from now). You may need to reschedule a meeting or two or delegate or simply live with the possibility that there may be some part of your life that is less excellent this week. If this feels foreign to you, remember that this is something you actually do every week already. It's just that you do it on the fly, later in the week, and (if you're like most of us) you wind up sacrificing your most important priorities.

○ Keep working on the filtering process until you have a
   schedule for the week that allows time for your most important priorities, time for current appointments and a
   few hours of margin.

DAY 10

What's My Job?

*Mystification is simple; clarity
is the hardest thing of all.*

JULIAN BARNES, *FLAUBERT'S PARROT*

Have you ever had a job that left you confused about exactly *what* you were supposed to be doing? If you're like most people, the result looked something like this:

- You were frustrated with the people who got you into the role to begin with.

- You felt like you were wasting your time.

- It is very likely that you would do everything in your power to prevent ever getting yourself into a situation like that again.

- The next time the person who got you into that role asks you to do something, you will be strongly inclined to say a resounding no.

Tragically, these bullet points describe how many (if not most) people who volunteer their time in the church often feel. They are asked to do something, pointed in a vague direction, and then left to figure it out on their own. As one volunteer said to us, "Around here, once you say yes, it's a life sentence."

But it doesn't have to be this way.

Providing each person on your team with a clear job description, including specific times you'll be meeting with them to clarify and recalibrate their roles, can make a world of difference. This one step may do more to increase the retention of your team members than any other idea you might try.

Today's Mission

1. Determine all the job descriptions you need for your ministry by making a list of all the positions, both volunteer and paid, that it will take to run your ministry effectively. Be sure to include paid staff and helpers (drivers, meal providers, etc.) as well as partners (small group leaders, Sunday school teachers, major event coordinators, etc.). Remember, at this point you're not only listing the positions you currently have but all those you hope to have in the coming year.

2. Identify the job descriptions that are your highest priority, likely the partner roles that you are spending time recruiting for right now.

3. Draft job descriptions for all your partner roles as well as for any paid staff in your ministry. Make sure you include how long the commitment is as well as the schedule of when meetings for coordination, planning and training will take place. (Job description sample templates are at ministryarchitects.com/30-day-change-resources.)

4. Meet face-to-face with any potential volunteers who have agreed to a meeting.

a. Bring the job description for the specific role for which you would like this person's help.

b. Begin the conversation by listening to your potential recruit to learn what they are thinking and feeling about the opportunity and to learn any concerns they might have.

c. Address their concerns with joyful clarity, being sure to ask for what you really need. It may be that at this point you discover you have someone willing to help but not someone willing to be a partner. If this is the case, do not slot this person into a partner role. Go back and find another person who might serve in the partner role, allowing this person to be a helper.

5. Continue your daily recruiting follow-up work:

a. Take out your master recruiting documents: your needs list and your ranked pool list.

b. Check your email to see if anyone has responded to your email invitation, and reply to those emails immediately.

c. For those who have said yes, send an email suggesting a meeting time and place for you to talk further about what you're looking for.

d. For those who have said no,

- Move their names to the bottom of the pool list, under the section called "No."

- Beside each name, write what role each person has said no to.

- Remove their names from the needs list.

e. Place new names in the blanks left by those who have said no.

f. Send your standard invitation email to the people you have added to your master recruiting list.

g. Follow up with those who have not responded to your first email (see appendix one for a sample of what your second contact might sound like).

 DAY 11

Ridiculous Lines from the Chronically Ineffective Leader

"It's Easier Just to Do It Myself"

*A leader is not an administrator who loves to run others,
but someone who carries water for his people
so that they can get on with their jobs.*

ROBERT TOWNSEND

When we find a church with an anemic volunteer leadership team, we don't have to look far before we stumble on to someone who lives by the motto, "It's easier just to do it myself!"

Well, of course it is. It's almost always easier simply to knock out a single task by ourselves than to have to coordinate with others. If easy is what we're looking for, it's actually easiest to do nothing at all!

But can we just agree that easy is not primarily what we're looking for?

Most of us, if we're willing to admit it, are like typical contestants on cable TV's design or food competitions. You don't have to watch long to realize that the *least* favorite challenges on these shows are the team competitions, the ones that require contestants to work together. There's a reason the contestants consistently hate these kinds of challenges. When it comes to creating or innovating, it's easier to do it alone than to have to compromise, co-create or share leadership with others.

Beyond the drama it creates, the judges on these shows have a purpose. They know from experience that the highest-level work, the most significant accomplishments in almost any field seldom happen by a single individual accomplishing a task. The greatest discoveries and most profound innovations take place as leaders build teams, not only beneath them but beside them and above them as well. In short, the greatest fruit in life and ministry might just come in the form of a "team challenge."

But we can't successfully lead a team until we have one, which is why you've made it a priority to build your team in this intense thirty-day challenge.

TODAY'S MISSION

1. Commit today to strike from your vocabulary as a leader the ridiculous line "It's just easier to do it myself."

2. Continue your daily recruiting follow-up work:

    a. Take out your master recruiting documents: your needs list and your ranked pool list.

    b. Check your email to see if anyone has responded to your email invitation, and reply to those emails immediately.

    c. For those who have said yes, send an email suggesting a meeting time and place for you to talk further about what you're looking for.

    d. Hold any scheduled meetings with potential volunteers.

e. For those who have said no,

- Move their names to the bottom of the pool list, under the section called "No."

- Beside each name, write what role each person has said no to.

- Remove their names from the needs list.

f. Place new names in the blanks left by those who have said no.

g. Send your standard invitation email to the people you have added to your master recruiting list.

h. Send a follow-up message to any potential volunteer who hasn't responded to your last message in three days or more.

3. Send an email or a text to confirm your upcoming meeting with your prayer partners.

 **DAY 12**

Ridiculous Lines from the Chronically Ineffective Leader

"I Called, but They Haven't Called Me Back Yet"

It's hard to beat a person who never gives up.

BABE RUTH

You may have found yourself uttering these ridiculous words yourself, after a week or so of calling and following up. Those new to leadership or new to building teams are often amazed— stunned— at how few potential volunteers respond after the first message.

Here's a good general rule: most *potential* team members won't call or email back after a single message. This rule is so true that there's a chance that the people who *do* call you back quickly after a single message may end up *not* being the kind of people you are looking for!

As an effective team builder, you should never be thrown off track by the slow response time of potential leaders. Instead, accept it as part of the landscape of building an effective team.

Each additional message you leave simply allows you to bring a little more enthusiasm and a little more detail to the conversation. You can say things like

- I'm thrilled about the possibility of someone like you working with our kids!

- We're looking at an hour and a half three Sundays a month during the school year.

- If you'd like to know more, you might want to talk with your good friends Jen and John who have been in this role for years and are fabulous!

Today you again get to lean into the bread and butter of building a great team—the follow-up process.

Today's Mission

1. Commit today to strike from your vocabulary as a leader the ridiculous line, "I've called, but they haven't called me back yet."

2. Continue your daily recruiting follow-up work:

   a. Take out your master recruiting documents: your needs list and your ranked pool list.

   b. Check your email to see if anyone has responded to your email invitation, and reply to those emails immediately.

   c. For those who have said yes, send an email suggesting a meeting time and place for you to talk further about what you're looking for.

   d. Hold any scheduled meetings with potential volunteers.

   e. For those who have said no,

      - Move their names to the bottom of the pool list, under the section called "No."

- Beside each name, write what role each person has said no to.

- Remove their names from the needs list.

f. Place new names in the blanks left by those who have said no.

g. Send your standard invitation email to the people you have added to your master recruiting list.

h. Send a follow-up message to any potential volunteer who hasn't responded to your last message in three days or more.

 **DAY 13**

Ridiculous Lines from the Chronically Ineffective Leader

"But I Don't Know Anyone to Ask"

*Leadership is getting people to help you
when they are not obligated to do so.*

JOHN C. MAXWELL

Every would-be team leader, salesperson or nonprofit director faces the same challenge: they don't know anyone else. It doesn't take long in the recruiting process before we run through our list of friends, family and acquaintances, and find ourselves saying, "I don't know anyone else."

But for the effective leader, this only means it is time for the next step. When we run out of people we know, we begin the process of building a team around something other than ourselves. And this, believe it or not, is a great thing.

When we get to this point, we can begin a deliberate sourcing process that increases our possible pool by tenfold or more. So today, in addition to your follow-up work, you'll return to the on-going leader's work, continuing the process of sourcing for additional people who might someday be on your team.

Today's Mission

1. Commit today to strike from your vocabulary as a leader the ridiculous line, "But I don't know anyone else!"

2. Rework your sourcing process:

   a. Contact five people in your church whom you may not know very well, let them know that you are in the process of building your youth ministry team for the coming year and ask if they have noticed anyone in the church who they think might have gifts for working with youth.

   b. Contact five parents of some of your more enthusiastically involved youth and ask them for the names of anyone they would recommend as a potential leader.

   c. Ask your colleagues on staff again for the names of any people they may not have thought of a couple weeks ago.

   d. Scan through the church directory to see if there might be someone there that you missed.

   e. Remember to look around on Sunday morning to see if there might be someone you may want to ask others in the congregation about.

   f. Add any new names to your master recruiting list and rank them (ABC, WEB) as you have ranked the others.

3. Continue your daily recruiting follow-up work:

   a. Take out your master recruiting documents: your needs list and your ranked pool list.

b. Check your email to see if anyone has responded to your email invitation, and reply to those emails immediately.

c. For those who have said yes, send an email suggesting a meeting time and place for you to talk further about what you're looking for.

d. Hold any scheduled meetings with potential volunteers.

e. For those who have said no,

- Move their names to the bottom of the pool list, under the section called "No."

- Beside each name, write what role each person has said no to.

- Remove their names from the needs list.

f. Place new names in the blanks left by those who have said no.

g. Send your standard invitation email to the people you have added to your master recruiting list.

h. Send a follow-up message to any potential volunteer who hasn't responded to your last message in three days or more.

 **DAY 14**

Ridiculous Lines from the Chronically Ineffective Leader

"What Do I Say on the Fourth Message?"

*Diligent follow-up and follow-through
will set you apart from the crowd
and communicate excellence.*

JOHN C. MAXWELL

By now, if you've been working this process faithfully, you're in one of two positions (maybe both):

- You're amazed by how many people have responded with an answer to the invitation to serve on your team, or

- You're wondering what in the world to say after being ignored despite multiple messages.

Good news! I'm including here on day fourteen eight different messages you can leave for those you're still waiting to hear from. My thought is that a message every three or four days gives your prospective leaders enough time between your calls, emails, texts or Facebook messages.

Here are the examples.

Message one: Hi Jill. It's Mark from church. I'm putting my team together to work with our seventh graders for next year, and I would love for you to think about being part of that group. Feel free to call me back with a "no" or a "maybe." If it's a maybe, let's get together and talk about it. If it's a no, I'll just call you in six months or a year to see if you might have seen a burning bush. My cell number is 555-5555 and my email address is Mark@yaya.com. Hope to hear from you soon.

Message two: Jill, it's Mark from church. Hope all is well in your world. I'm just circling around to see what you're thinking about the possibility of working with our seventh graders starting in the fall. You would be terrific! Feel free to call (555-5555) or email (Mark@yaya.com) any time. Have a great rest of the day!

Message three: Hey Jill, let me tell you why I'm excited! I'm excited because you haven't given me a "no" yet about working with our seventh graders. I'm thrilled you're still thinking about it! Give me a call whenever it's convenient for you (555-5555).

Message four: Hi Jill, it's your old friend Mark from church! You'll be thrilled to know that _____ has agreed to work with our new seventh graders starting in the fall. I think you guys would work beautifully together. You can just call me back with a "no" or a "maybe." If it's a maybe, I'd love to buy you some coffee and talk further. If it's a no, I'll ask about something else another time! My email is Mark@yaya.com.

Message five: Jill, my friend! I know your life is crazy right now, but I'm encouraged that I haven't heard a "no" from you yet! Our team really feels that you have the kind of gifts and personality and faith that we'd love for our seventh graders to be around. I look forward to hearing from you soon at 555-5555 or Mark@yaya.com. If I don't hear back from you in a couple days, I'll just call back.

Message six: Jill, are you feeling the love? It's Mark. Hopefully, you've heard in my previous messages how excited we'd be to have you on our team with our new seventh graders. I'm sure you've got a few questions. Just give me a call or an email, and you can give me a little clarity about what you're thinking: 555-5555 or Mark@yaya.com.

Message seven: Hi Jill! It's Mark. I'm here with our youth group right now. And they've got something to say to you [insert cacophony of kids yelling things like "You'll be great!" "Thanks for thinking about us!" "We want you!" all at the same time]. Great to be wanted, isn't it? Hope to hear from you soon. You've got my contact info, or you can just leave a message at the church on my voicemail at 222-2222.

Message eight: Okay, Jill. I'm not beyond bribery. How about you let me buy you lunch and we talk about this whole seventh grade leader thing. Let me know a good time for you. Mark@yaya.com. Have a great day!

You've probably noticed a pattern in these messages, a pattern that reveals three keys to great follow-up:

- Consistency: They'll soon realize that they'll be hearing back from you in a few days.

- Brevity: The messages need to be short. All you're trying to do is to see if she's interested in a conversation. If she is, you can give more detail at that point.

- Enthusiasm: You gain nothing by being grumpy and complaining that you haven't heard back.

With 90 percent of the folks you recruit, you won't need to leave more than five messages. But for that other 10 percent, you've now got a starting point for all the messages you'll be leaving.

TODAY'S MISSION

1. Confirm your next meeting with your prayer partners for this project.

2. Because you'll be taking the next two days off from active recruitment and follow-up, today is the day to get your master recruiting list completely up to date.

   a. Add to your master recruiting list any additional names of potential volunteers that might have bubbled up in your sourcing process.

   b. Make sure everyone on your pool list is appropriately categorized:

      - Those who have said no are taken out of the master list and put at the bottom of the list, each with a note indicating what roles they said no to.

      - Those you're still waiting to hear back from are highlighted in some way, with indications for each of how many messages you have left.

      - Those who have said yes are written into your master needs list in big, black marker.

3. Continue your daily recruiting follow-up work:

    a. With your master recruiting documents (your needs list and your ranked pool list) in front of you, check your email to see if anyone has responded to your invitation and reply to those emails immediately.

    b. For those who have said yes, make sure their names are written in black ink on your master list.

    c. For those who have said maybe, send an email suggesting a meeting time and place for you to talk further about what you're looking for.

    d. Hold any scheduled meetings with potential volunteers.

    e. For those who have said no,

- Move their names to the bottom of the pool list, under the section called "No."

- Beside each name, write what role each person has said no to.

- Remove their names from the needs list.

- Place new names in the blanks left by those who have said no.

    f. Send your standard invitation email to the people you have added to your master recruiting list.

    g. Send a follow-up message to any potential volunteer who hasn't responded to your last message in three days or more.

 **DAY 15**

Reflection Day

Elisha's Eyes

And Elisha prayed, "Open his eyes, LORD, so that he may see."
Then the LORD opened the servant's eyes, and he looked and saw
the hills full of horses and chariots of fire all around Elisha.

2 KINGS 6:17

Some days, it's helpful to remember that we're not alone in this battle. Today is one of those days.

This is your sabbath day, not a day to climb or strive or gut it out. It is a day to rest in the confidence that this is God's work, even when (maybe especially when) we can't see the results we want. While you rest, trust that God is busy at work behind the scenes, stirring and wooing those you have invited to join you in ministry with God's kids.

Feel free to reflect on and pray through the questions under To-day's Mission, or simply wait to talk them through with your prayer partners when you meet in a few days. You've already scheduled

your next meeting with your prayer partners, so take the freedom
to fully detach and unplug from this project today.

Regardless, catch your breath and rest in the certainty that God is
at work when we are not. May God bless you with the eyes of Elisha,
who could see God's Spirit at work when others were blind to it.

TODAY'S MISSION

1. Send a text to your prayer partners just saying thanks for joining
   you in this process.

2. When you meet with your prayer partners,

   a. Share with them your answers to these questions:

   - What are you most excited about, after having
     worked this process now for two weeks?

   - What has been your biggest point of discouragement?

   - As you look at the next week, what times have you set
     aside to focus on the assignments you've been given?

   - How can your prayer partners be praying for you this
     week, whether about this 30-Day Change process or
     about anything else that you're experiencing as par-
     ticularly pressing at this point in your life?

   b. Share with your prayer partners your updated master recruiting documents.

   c. Pray together over the names of the folks you will particularly be focusing on this week and about any challenges you are facing in this process.

 **DAY 16**

Balcony Day

Procrastinate Now!

Someone who is busier than you
found time to exercise right now.

SOMETHING I READ ON THE WINDOW OF A GYM
WHILE I WAS ON MY WAY TO LUNCH

I procrastinate every day. And I'm proud of it. I want you to be a procrastinator too.

I'm proud of being a procrastinator. In fact, it's the key to the 30-Day Change program, even the key to progress in any area of our lives.

If you have never perfected the skill of procrastination, you'll spend as much time every day on secondary priorities as you do on primary ones. Today (and every day), try procrastinating (guilt free) on any priority that is not the most important thing for you to be doing *right now*.

Sounds easy, but as you know it can be mighty hard. Most people never take the time each week, then each day, to determine what those things are that will make their lives different a year from now.

And as a result, they procrastinate on all the wrong things.

Your balcony time is likely the most important time you'll spend this week. This is the time you'll spend triaging everything on your to-do list and selecting those things that are mission critical for your life and future. Your top priorities are not to be confused with your screaming, urgent priorities. Your top priorities are those that move you closer to the life you want by focusing on the right things today.

As a refresher on how this process works, you can look back at day nine. This will help you do a weekly review and identify your most important priorities for the week. During this balcony day, also make time to troubleshoot any challenges you've had to doing the most important things first, especially the daily priorities outlined in this project.

Remember, it's on the days that you fail to procrastinate well that you'll get into the most trouble. Refuse to just fire up the computer and go after emails without thinking. *Decide* first what your top priorities will be, and put at least one of those on the top of each day's to-do list.

Procrastinate on everything else.

Today's Mission

1. Make an updated master list of all those who have said yes to specific roles. Print out that list, including the role that each person has agreed to, and display it prominently in your office.

2. Take a look at your task list for the week (or create one if this is not a natural part of the rhythm of your life yet). Identify your top priorities for the week. You are looking here for things that will make your life and ministry more the way you'd like them to be a year from now (not to be confused with the screaming, urgent demands on your time). Your top priorities might include

   o deliberate time with your family,

   o time for specific spiritual disciplines

○ and (of course) during these thirty days, two hours daily focused on building your volunteer team.

3. Complete your calendar for the week, including all currently scheduled appointments (including meetings, programs and any other commitments). Now make appointments with yourself for your top priorities identified in step two.

4. As was the case last week, you may find that, when you add your currently scheduled commitments and your top priorities, you are already out of time for the week (and you still have a few urgent things you've got to get to, not to mention returning emails and messages). On some weeks this is *normal*. If this is the case for you this week, you've got some problem solving to do. Here's a start:

○ Corral your emails and phone calls into a specific time block for each day. If your week is packed, you simply don't have time to be immediately available this week.

○ Determine what will need to be cut from your schedule, being careful not to cut any of your top priorities (those things that have the potential to make your life and ministry different a year from now).

○ You may need to reschedule a meeting or two or delegate or simply live with the possibility that there may be some part of your life that is less excellent this week. If this feels foreign to you, remember that this is something you *already do* every week. It's just that you do it on the fly, later in the week, and (if you're like most of us) you wind up sacrificing your most important priorities.

○ Keep working on the filtering process until you have a schedule for the week that allows time for your most important priorities, time for current appointments and a few hours of margin.

 **DAY 17**

Your Leader's Calendar

You will never find time for anything.
If you want time, you must make it.

CHARLES BUXTON

I'm going to venture a pretty safe wager. If you haven't calendared time to develop your volunteer leaders, I'm going to bet that it just hasn't happened.

Many youth pastors I know get discouraged. They say things like, "I plan these leader meetings, and only a third of my leaders actually show up! I really don't think it's worth it!"

Do you know what we call it when a third of the leaders show up for the first year of leader meetings? We call it "normal."

You don't have to hold a meeting every week or even every month to have an effective, well-equipped team. But you do need a plan that includes time scheduled for you to invest in your leaders. To make that plan, you can start by answering five pre-calendaring questions:

- How often do you want your leaders to be together, just as leaders, over the span of a year?

- What would you like to do for an orientation for your leaders at the beginning of the year?

- When would you like to celebrate the work the leaders have done at the end of the year?

- What would you like to do to ensure that the leaders who can't (or won't) make the meetings have access to the training and the sense of connection that will take place at the meeting?

- Are there any other special times you'd like your team to be together, such as a Christmas party, a commissioning service or a community training you'd like to promote?

If regular leader meetings are new for you, don't get paralyzed by the need to get the plan perfect. The key this year is simply to have a plan and to translate that plan into your calendar.

Today's Mission

1. Answer the five pre-calendaring questions above. At this point, don't worry too much about what's realistic. Start with what you'd love to see happen in terms of the rhythm of your leader gatherings.

2. Pull out your master ministry calendar for the coming year. (If you don't have one yet, this would be a good time to create the first draft of such a thing.) Most youth pastors choose to schedule their leader events from August or September of the coming year through July or August of the next year. Ideally, you want to start with a calendar that (1) enables you to look at the entire year at one time and (2) includes key programming and holidays for the entire year.

3. With a *pencil*, schedule leader gatherings for the coming year, prompted by the five pre-calendaring questions.

4. Once you've got all the dates on the calendar based on your responses to the pre-calendaring questions, look at the flow of the ministry year and make adjustments as needed. For example, on closer examination you may discover that you've planned a leader dinner for Super Bowl Sunday, or you've planned your big leader orientation meeting on a Saturday morning that conflicts with a school fundraiser in your town. Make adjustments as needed.

5. Check in with two or three of your current key volunteers: email them a copy of your calendar and gather their feedback on your leader-development calendar for the coming year. Make adjustments to the calendar based on their feedback.

6. In the meantime, of course, you'll continue your recruiting and follow-up work:

   a. With your master recruiting documents (your needs list and your ranked pool list) in front of you, check your email to see if anyone has responded to your invitation and reply to those emails immediately.

   b. For those who have said yes, make sure their names are written in black ink on your master list.

   c. For those who have said maybe, send an email suggesting a meeting time and place for you to talk further about what you're looking for.

   d. Hold any scheduled meetings with potential volunteers.

   e. For those who have said no,

      • Move their names to the bottom of the pool list, under the section called "No."

      • Beside each name, write what role each person has said no to.

- Remove their names from the needs list.

- Place new names in the blanks left by those who have said no.

f. Send your standard invitation email to the people you have added to your master recruiting list.

g. Send a follow-up message to any potential volunteer who hasn't responded to your last message in three days or more.

 **DAY 18**

Preparing Your Leader Documents

> *Champions do not become champions when they win the event,*
> *but in the hours, weeks, months and years they spend*
> *preparing for it. The victorious performance itself*
> *is merely the demonstration of their*
> *championship character.*
>
> ALAN ARMSTRONG

Before your next year's leadership team assembles for the first time, you'll need a few key documents in place. These documents will not only give your leaders ready access to the information they will need to play their positions well, it will also instill confidence that yours is the kind of ministry that will not be a waste of their time.

When a new leader begins in our ministries with nothing more concrete than "you'll mostly just figure it out as you go along" and a pat on the back, we shouldn't be surprised that people don't naturally want to volunteer and that those who do don't stay for long. Follow this checklist and you'll give your leaders (and yourself) a huge head start:

- Compile and print a directory of all your volunteer leaders, including their contact information and the roles each person will be playing. Make sure to include your youth ministry website and your inner-circle contact information. Download a sample directory at ministryarchitects.com/30-day-change-resources.

- Compile and print your major event calendar for the coming year, including not only your ministry's major events but also major events for the entire church, as well as holidays and key school events (graduations, etc.). For a sample major event calendar, see appendix two.

- Compile and print an accurate directory of students to give to your leaders. This should include contact information, grade level, parents' names and contact information, schools and any other information unique to your ministry. Download a sample youth directory at ministryarchitects.com/30-day-change-resources.

- Compile and print child protection forms, safe sanctuary policies or lifestyle covenants that give clear expectations (for example, is it okay for a leader to drive a student alone in his or her car? Take a student to an R-rated movie? Drink alcohol or smoke on a youth retreat? View pornography on his or her own time?). Download a sample child protection/safe sanctuary template at ministryarchitects.com/30-day-change-resources.

- Compile and print job descriptions for each of the volunteers who will be serving in the ministry. Download sample job descriptions at ministryarchitects.com/30-day-change-resources.

- Compile all the documents you will need for your leader orientation.

Unless you've already completed these documents, you will likely not have time to complete the entire checklist today in the time you've allotted for the 30-Day Change project. Your mission today will be to begin the processes that will ensure that all these documents are in place before your thirty days are up.

Today's Mission

1. Take at least one step for each of the five leader documents below. This could mean starting the work yourself or assigning a partner to complete the document in the next ten days.

   - youth leader directory
   - major event calendar
   - youth directory
   - child protection and screening forms and policies
   - job descriptions

2. Continue your daily recruiting and follow-up work:

   a. With your master recruiting documents (your needs list and your ranked pool list) in front of you, check your email to see if anyone has responded to your invitation and reply to those emails immediately.

   b. For those who have said yes, make sure their names are written in black ink on your master list.

   c. For those who have said maybe, send an email suggesting a meeting time and place for you to talk further about what you're looking for.

   d. Hold any scheduled meetings with potential volunteers.

   e. For those who have said no,

      - Move their names to the bottom of the pool list, under the section called "No."

      - Beside each name, write what role each person has said no to.

- Remove their names from the needs list.

- Place new names in the blanks left by those who have said no.

f. Send your standard invitation email to the people you have added to your master recruiting list.

g. Send a follow-up message to any potential volunteer who hasn't responded to your last message in three days or more.

3. Send an email or a text to confirm your upcoming meeting with your prayer partners.

 **DAY 19**

Structuring Your Team for Maximum Impact

*80 percent of your problems are not people problems,
they are system problems. . . . Your ministry is
perfectly designed to get the results it's getting.*

ANDY STANLEY

You are working really hard during these thirty days to make sure you are getting the "right people on the bus" for your ministry.[1] Today, you'll look into whether you've got the right people in the right seats on the bus.

Enthusiasm, of course, is contagious. When you have volunteer leaders who absolutely *love* what they are doing in the youth ministry, they will not only be satisfied and exceptionally effective, they will also be magnets to others like them.

Not every leader will be a fit. Some will do a fine job but out of obligation. Others will be so overwhelmed with challenges in their personal lives that the possibility of them having a life-giving volunteer experience is minimal. For these kinds of people, there may not be much you can do.

But for many (if not most) volunteers, you can do a lot to position them for maximum satisfaction in their roles. Today's mission starts you on that process.

TODAY'S MISSION

1. Pull out the list of all your current leaders and rank each of their satisfaction levels related to their role in the ministry, as you imagine it.

   o **A rank of 1** means that they are doing work that makes their heart sing, and they come away from their work in your ministry almost always grateful and delighted to have served.

   o **A rank of 2** means that they feel their work is making a difference and they are committed to it, even if at times it feels like an obligation.

   o **A rank of 3** means that they are willing to keep their commitment for this year but will probably quit at the end of the year. They have determined that the payoff is not worth their investment.

   o **A rank of 4** means that they are unhappy in their roles and likely to drop out soon, if changes aren't made.

   o **A rank of 5** means you have no idea how satisfied they are in their roles.

2. For those with a rank of 5, give them a call or send them an email and ask them to rank themselves according to one of the first four categories.

3. Draft an organizational chart for your ministry. Make sure that it is easily editable and that it clearly shows who is responsible for what *and* who is responsible if that person doesn't get his or her job done. Remember, this is not so much a program description

chart as it is a responsibility chart. For sample youth ministry organizational charts, go to ministryarchitects.com/30-day -change-resources.

4. Continue your recruiting and follow-up work:

    a. With your master recruiting documents (your needs list and your ranked pool list) in front of you, check your email to see if anyone has responded to your email invitation and reply to those emails immediately.

    b. For those who have said yes, make sure their names are written in black ink on your master list.

    c. For those who have said maybe, send an email suggesting a meeting time and place for you to talk further about what you're looking for.

    d. Hold any scheduled meetings with potential volunteers.

    e. For those who have said no,

- Move their names to the bottom of the pool list, under the section called "No."

- Beside each name, write what role each person has said no to.

- Remove their names from the needs list.

- Place new names in the blanks left by those who have said no.

    f. Send your standard invitation email to the people you have added to your master recruiting list.

    g. Send a follow-up message to any potential volunteer who hasn't responded to your last message in three days or more.

5. Take one more step for each of the five leader documents below, either working on the document yourself or checking in with

the person responsible to complete the document in the next nine days.

- o youth leader directory
- o major event calendar
- o youth directory
- o child protection and screening forms and policies
- o job descriptions

 **DAY 20**

The Magic in the Middle

Drudgery is the touchstone of faithfulness.

OSWALD CHAMBERS

As of today, you are two-thirds of the way through your thirty-day experiment. You have done some heavy lifting up to this point, and we've thrown a lot at you.

Here's the good news: today you will not be adding anything *new* to your task list for this project. Instead, you will continue to work the process. We call it "the magic in the middle." Seth Godin calls it "drip by drip." The magic in the middle comes only after the novelty has worn off and you simply continue your "long obedience in the same direction" (thanks, Eugene Peterson).

Though there's nothing particularly fresh or exciting about the tasks you'll be doing in these middle-magic days, managing them well will secure the trajectory of change that got you into this thirty-day adventure in the first place.

So when you start to feel discouraged or bored with repetition, keep reminding yourself that the magic is what happens in the middle. Though novelty may be the controlling value for most people, you're going countercultural—not doing anything new, not chasing after the latest quick fix, not adding anything to your list.

Today, you will make a little slow and steady progress.

Enjoy the magic.

TODAY'S MISSION

1. Continue your recruiting and follow-up work:

   a. With your master recruiting documents (your needs list and your ranked pool list) in front of you, check your email to see if anyone has responded to your invitation and reply to those emails immediately.

   b. For those who have said yes, make sure their names are written in black ink on your master list.

   c. For those who have said maybe, send an email suggesting a meeting time and place for you to talk further about what you're looking for.

   d. Hold any scheduled meetings with potential volunteers.

   e. For those who have said no,

   - Move their names to the bottom of the pool list, under the section called "No."

   - Beside each name, write what role each person has said no to.

   - Remove their names from the needs list.

   - Place new names in the blanks left by those who have said no.

   f. Send your standard invitation email to the people you have added to your master recruiting list.

   g. Send a follow-up message to any potential volunteer who hasn't responded to your last message in three days or more.

2. Take one more step for each of the five leader documents below,
   either working on the document yourself or checking in with
   the person responsible to complete the document in the next
   eight days.

   ○ youth leader directory

   ○ major event calendar

   ○ youth directory

   ○ child protection and screening forms and policies

   ○ job descriptions

 DAY 21

Running Through the Wall

It's a little like wrestling a gorilla.
You don't quit when you're tired.
You quit when the gorilla is tired.

ROBERT STRAUSS

I (Nate) love running marathons. But, between you and me, I could do without miles seventeen to twenty-one. When the gun sounds at the beginning of a marathon, the streets are surging with life, with energy, with novelty. Buoyed by screaming crowds, blasting music and tens of thousands of people all running in the same direction, most runners find the first ten miles a breeze.

But about the time mile thirteen comes around, the half-marathoners have peeled off, reducing the number of runners by more than 75 percent, and the crowd has thinned to a sparse collection of friends and family. Only the most dedicated fans climb their way to those out-of-the-way parts of the route on the backside of the race. After mile fifteen, things start to get a little (okay, a lot) lonelier.

For me, mile seventeen always seems to be the toughest. I've still got more than nine miles to go. My body is tired, my legs feel heavy and sore, and I begin to question my sanity and whether I've got what it takes to put one foot in front of the other for almost two more grueling hours (yeah, I'm *that* fast). Once I've passed the twenty-one-mile mark, I know I can gut it out until the end, but miles seventeen through twenty-one are where I most want to quit.

Today, you may find yourself in just this slice of your 30-Day Change project. If you do, you may have found your mind is starting to play tricks on you. You think, *I keep plugging away, and nothing is working,* or *There are so many urgent things to attend to, I can't keep spending this amount of time on just one priority.*

And you would be normal.

No one makes it to the finish line (in your case, to an entirely new culture with a full volunteer team in place) without passing through miles seventeen to twenty-one. During these days, don't get caught in the whirlpool of too much thinking about why. Just put one foot in front of the other, put in the time, and in less than ten days you'll see that finish line.

Today's Mission

1. Continue your recruiting and follow-up work:

   a. With your master recruiting documents (your needs list and your ranked pool list) in front of you, check your email to see if anyone has responded to your invitation and reply to those emails immediately.

   b. For those who have said yes, make sure their names are written in black ink on your master list.

   c. For those who have said maybe, send an email suggesting a meeting time and place for you to talk further about what you're looking for.

    d. Hold any scheduled meetings with potential volunteers.

    e. For those who have said no,

- Move their names to the bottom of the pool list, under the section called "No."

- Beside each name, write what role each person has said no to.

- Remove their names from the needs list.

- Place new names in the blanks left by those who have said no.

    f. Send your standard invitation email to the people you have added to your master recruiting list.

    g. Send a follow-up message to any potential volunteer who hasn't responded to your last message in three days or more.

2. Take one more step for each of the five leader documents below, either working on the document yourself or checking in with the person responsible to complete the document in the next seven days.

- youth leader directory
- major event calendar
- youth directory
- child protection and screening forms and policies
- job descriptions

3. Take a look at the structure document you developed on day nineteen. Using the ranked list of your current volunteers, determine if anyone is in the "wrong seat on the bus." Make one step today toward moving someone on your current team into a role that will be more life-giving for the volunteer and more impactful for your ministry.

 **DAY 22**

Reflection Day

Trusting Versus Trudging

In quietness and trust is your strength.

ISAIAH 30:15

This past week you have been plodding it out, faithfully tending to the very unexciting tasks of follow-up and tracking and clarifying—and following up again.

Today you take a break from the trudging, from the fruitful discipline of persistence. This is your sabbath day, a day different from the others in the week. It's a day to remember that the real work of transformation rests in God's hands, not in your muscles. Today is a day to rest in the confidence that this is, fundamentally, God's work. While you rest today, trust that God continues to work behind the scenes, putting together a team to join you in ministry.

Feel free to reflect on and pray through the questions under Today's Mission, or simply wait to talk them through with your prayer partners when you meet in a few days. You've already scheduled your next meeting with your prayer partners, so take the freedom to fully detach and unplug from this project today.

Regardless, take some time to be quiet. In the silence, imagine trust growing in you as an unseen seed underground. Knowing that your strength is limited, rest today in God's.

Today's Mission

1. Send a text to your prayer partners just saying thanks for joining you in this process.

2. When you meet with your prayer partners,

   a. Share with them the answers to these questions:

      • What are you most excited about after having worked this process for three weeks?

      • What has been your biggest point of discouragement?

      • As you look at the next week, what times have you set aside to focus on the assignments you've been given?

      • How can your prayer partners be praying for you this week, whether about this 30-Day Change process or about anything else that you're experiencing as particularly pressing at this point in your life?

   b. Share with your prayer partners the updated master recruiting documents you've been using this past week.

   c. Pray together over the names of the folks you will particularly be focusing on this week and about any challenges you are facing in this process.

 **DAY 23**

Balcony Day

Finishing Well

Teach us to number our days,
that we may gain a heart of wisdom.

PSALM 90:12

Tomorrow begins your last week of the 30-Day Change project. Today you will work from thirty thousand feet, working *on* this project, not just *in* it. Today you will do the essential work of ordering your final week for maximum impact. Today you get to bring order to your worksite as you move into the final stage, which we call "finishing well." Today you will pull together the loose ends and set the stage for a profound transformation in the culture of your ministry.

As I wrote the words "profound transformation," I had to pause and wonder, "Am I just being dramatic, or are those words actually true?"

I'm sticking with those words: profound transformation.

Here's why: though the change may feel imperceptible to you, the shift from having an anemic, bare-bones volunteer team to having all your players in place is nothing short of *profound*. Seeing a solid volunteer infrastructure where there was none is like looking at a vineyard where there was a vacant lot or at a new home where there once was a dilapidated trailer.

There's a good chance that over the last twenty-two days you have accomplished *most* of the assignments in this book. But there's an even better chance that some have been left undone. Maybe you left some assignments 80 percent complete, but there's still that 20 percent awaiting your attention.

You've got eight days to complete this transforming project, so let's dive into today's mission.

TODAY'S MISSION

1. Begin by taking stock of any loose ends from the past twenty-two days.

   o Review the daily assignments from the past twenty-two days.

   o Create a written list of all the items that still remain incomplete.

   o For each item on the "remaining items" list, estimate how much time it will take to complete.

   o Knowing that you really have six days left to complete these outstanding tasks, schedule time to complete each of them during the coming week. Once you have determined how much time each task will require, add 20 percent to that number of minutes and schedule those times in your calendar.

   o Repeat this process for these newly found items as a part

of Today's Mission on days twenty-four through thirty.

2. Update your master recruiting list.

    o Make an updated master list of all those who have said yes to specific roles. Print out that list, including the role that each person has agreed to play, and display it prominently in your office.

    o Summarize on one sheet of paper the roles that are yet to be filled. For this last week, you will be working from this much shorter list.

    o Place a different potential volunteer's name in each of the blanks for the remaining roles, using the remaining names on your master recruiting list as your pool.

3. Take a look at your task list for the week. Identify your top priorities for the week. You are looking here for things that will make your life and ministry more the way you'd like them to be a year from now (not the screaming, urgent demands on your time). Your top priorities might include

    o deliberate time with your family,

    o time for specific spiritual disciplines

    o and (of course) during this last week, two hours daily focused on building your volunteer team.

4. Complete your calendar for the week, including all currently scheduled appointments (including meetings, programs and any other commitments). Now make appointments with yourself for your top priorities you identified in step three above.

5. You may very well find that when you add your currently scheduled commitments and top priorities, you are already out of time for the week (and you still have a few urgent things

you've got to get to, not to mention returning emails and messages). On some weeks this is *normal*. If this is the case for you this week, you've got some problem solving to do. Here's a start:

o Corral your emails and phone calls into a specific time block for each day. If your week is packed, you simply don't have time to be immediately available this week. Plan on taking a break from Facebook and Twitter as well.

o Determine what will need to be cut from your schedule, being careful not to cut any of your top priorities (those things that have the potential to make your life and ministry different a year from now). You may need to reschedule a meeting or two or delegate some tasks or simply live with the possibility that there may be some part of your life that is less excellent this week. Remember that making these schedule and expectation adjustments for the upcoming week now prevents you from sacrificing more important priorities later.

o Keep working on the filtering process until you have a schedule for the week that allows time for your most important priorities, time for current appointments and a few hours of margin.

DAY 24

A Matter of Time

Give, and it will be given to you.

LUKE 6:38

I've learned a secret about writing: put in the time, and you'll have a book. The reason most people who say they want to be writers don't get their book written is not because they don't have the ability. It's almost always because they don't put in the time.

This book is a cousin of "Write a Novel in Thirty Days," giving you the steps to transform the volunteer culture around your youth ministry. Our experience is that those who put in the time have all the volunteers they need. Those who don't put in the time complain about how unsupportive their churches are.

As you may know, I (Mark) have publically made a one hundred dollar bet with thousands of people. Here's the challenge I've made: "If you will use the recruiting method I teach, spending at least two hours a day, five days a week for six months, and you don't have all the volunteers you need at the end of that six months, I'll pay you one hundred dollars."

I've never *once* had to pay.

Though I think the process clearly works, I'm afraid the bigger reason I've never lost the bet is that most people just don't put in the time. The hard part is not knowing what to do; it's doing it. It's a matter of time. If we work the process, the process just works. Give the necessary time to this project, and the time you give will be given back to you in the form of partners who multiply your ministry by helping you carry the load.

Today's Mission

1. Take one more step for each of the five leader documents, either working on the document yourself or providing support to the person responsible to complete the document in the next four days:

   o youth leader directory

   o major event calendar

   o youth directory

   o child protection and screening forms and policies

   o job descriptions

2. Take a look at the structure document or organizational chart that you developed on day nineteen. Using the ranked list of your current volunteers, determine if anyone is in the "wrong seat on the bus." Make one step today toward moving someone on your current team into a role that will be more life-giving for the volunteer and more impactful for your ministry.

3. Complete the items you've assigned yourself to accomplish on this day. If you haven't scheduled specific items on this day, return to day twenty-three and complete step one.

4. Develop your potential helper list, drawing on the names of those who have said no to a specific partner role but who you think might be willing to serve in a one-time helper role sometime during the year.

5. Edit the helper role survey, which includes a sample list of helper roles, to personalize it for your church. It can be found in appendix three and at ministryarchitects.com/30-day -change-resources.

6. Continue your recruiting and follow-up work:

    a. With your master recruiting documents (your needs list and your ranked pool list) in front of you, check your email to see if anyone has responded to your invitation, and reply to those emails immediately.

    b. For those who have said yes, make sure their names are written in black ink on your master list.

    c. For those who have said maybe, send an email suggesting a meeting time and place for you to talk further about what you're looking for.

    d. Hold any scheduled meetings with potential volunteers.

    e. For those who have said no,

- Move their names to the bottom of the pool list, under the section called "No."

- Beside each name, write what role each person has said no to.

- Remove their names from the needs list.

- Place new names in the blanks left by those who have said no.

    f. Send your standard invitation email to the people you have added to your master recruiting list.

    g. Send a follow-up message to any potential volunteer who hasn't responded to your last message in three days or more.

 **DAY 25**

Volunteers with a Twist

A foolish consistency is the hobgoblin of little minds.

RALPH WALDO EMERSON

You've now had enough face-to-face meetings with potential volunteers that you've learned that some of your best volunteers will want to say "yes," but with a twist.

Maybe your potential recruit is a doctor who is on call every third weekend and can't guarantee she'll be there every week. Maybe you're talking to someone with an aging parent whose unplanned emergencies may pull this leader away at the last minute. Maybe you've got a college student who will be gone during the summers and holidays.

Most of your volunteers will bring their own unique twist to what they are able to do. Here are a few principles to guide you as you put your "twisted" team together:

- You are building *a team* (not recruiting a single superstar), so the fact that your team members all have different needs is just a part of the fabric, not a reason for panic. Just because someone has a special situation does not mean that they can't play a partner role.

- In this part of the process, you are building a team of *partners*. Remember, partners are folks who will take initiative and take care of their responsibilities without you reminding them. This means, for example, that they adjust their teaching rotation among themselves, or they communicate to their youth directly without expecting every announcement to come through you.

- Be careful that you never slot a helper (someone waiting for you—or someone else—to take the initiative) into a partner role. If you do, you'll be a miserable manager, always complaining about your volunteers' lack of commitment. When someone says, "I can't commit to every week, but just call me when you have a need and I might be able to step in," that person is a helper, not to be included as a partner on the team.

As you build your team, you will quickly learn that some of your very best partners are those with whom you'll need to do the twist. So be firm in your need for partners, not just helpers, but be flexible enough to be creative when a potential A-player volunteer needs it.

Today's Mission

1. Complete the items you've assigned yourself to accomplish on this day. If you haven't scheduled specific items on this day, return to day twenty-three and complete step one.

2. Continue your recruiting and follow-up work:

   a. With your master recruiting documents (your needs list and your ranked pool list) in front of you, check your email to see if anyone has responded to your invitation and reply to those emails immediately.

b. For those who have said yes, make sure their names are written in black ink on your master list.

c. For those who have said maybe, send an email suggesting a meeting time and place for you to talk further about what you're looking for.

d. Hold any scheduled meetings with potential volunteers.

e. For those who have said no,

- Move their names to the bottom of the pool list, under the section called "No."

- Beside each name, write what role each person has said no to.

- Remove their names from the needs list.

- Place new names in the blanks left by those who have said no.

f. Send your standard invitation email to the people you have added to your master recruiting list.

g. Send a follow-up message to any potential volunteer who hasn't responded to your last message in three days or more.

3. Take one more step for each of the five leader documents, either working on the document yourself or providing support to the person responsible to complete the document in the next three days:

- youth leader directory

- major event calendar

- youth directory

- child protection and screening forms and policies

- job descriptions

4. Take a look at the structure document you developed on day nineteen. Using the ranked list of your current volunteers, determine if anyone is in the "wrong seat on the bus." Make one step today toward moving someone on your current team into a role that will be more life-giving for the volunteer and more impactful for your ministry.

5. Send an email to all your potential helpers with the survey you edited yesterday. You can use the "sample email to potential helpers" on the next page as a starting point.

6. Send an email or a text to confirm your upcoming meeting with your prayer partners.

Sample email to potential helpers

Dear [NAME],

As we launch into our fall program, we are thrilled to let you know that we have a marvelous team of leaders serving in our youth ministry this year. Over [NUMBER] members of our church family will be playing significant roles with our students, some working weekly with them and others working behind the scenes (I've attached a list of this great group who will be serving this year).

Though all our major volunteer responsibilities are covered, there are a few areas where those who have agreed to serve will need a little help. That's where you come in.

We are hoping that all of our parents will be able to do something in our youth ministry in the coming year—maybe driving for an event, helping with setup or cleanup, bringing cookies or helping out with decorations. We hope that at least once during the year you'd be willing to be one of our youth ministry helpers.

I'm attaching a survey of helper opportunities. You should be able to complete it in less than three minutes, and you can then email or mail it back to us. We'll be in touch with you when an opportunity comes up that matches your interest. It's as simple as that.

Thanks for your willingness to partner with us in this work that we get to do with all of our kids.

Blessings,

[NAME]

[TITLE]

 **DAY 26**

Architecting a New Culture

Come, let us rebuild . . .

NEHEMIAH 2:17

Y ou can be a victim of the culture of your ministry, or the architect of it. Architecting the culture of your ministry begins with putting in writing, as clearly as possible, what you want to see. But that step is only the beginning—the right beginning, but only a beginning.

Most mission statements fail to set the direction for their ministries. Why? Most mission statements take months to be formulated and weeks to be laminated and hung, but almost no time to fall behind the piano, only to be found years later at the church's once-a-decade cleaning event. Writing a goal statement about volunteers is not enough to change the culture. A nice goal document combined with a healthy dose of hoping, wishing and praying will, more often than not, leave you still feeling like a victim of a culture you can't control.

But you have chosen to do it differently. You have spent the last twenty-five days architecting your team, intentionally working the process that will not simply get new volunteers on board but will, ultimately, change the culture of your ministry.

With just a few days of this culture-changing boot camp left, we hope you're beginning to actually feel something different—a change in you as well as in your ministry.

Today's Mission

1. Complete the items you've assigned yourself to accomplish on this day. If you haven't scheduled specific items on this day, return to day twenty-three and complete step one.

2. If you haven't done this already, develop a calendar for how you will spread the viral good news about the strong youth ministry volunteer team in place for the coming year. Consider including the following actions:

    o Celebrate the new volunteer team in the church newsletter.

    o Report the names and roles of your new volunteer team to the church's leadership.

    o Have a special program for the youth (and their parents) at which the new volunteers are celebrated and introduced.

    o Commission the volunteer team before the congregation.

    o Write an article for your church's website about the new team of volunteers.

    o Introduce and celebrate your new team of volunteers on the youth ministry's Facebook page.

3. Continue your recruiting and follow-up work:

    a. With your master recruiting documents (your needs list and your ranked pool list) in front of you, check your email to see if anyone has responded to your invitation and reply to those emails immediately.

b. For those who have said yes, make sure their names are written in black ink on your master list.

c. For those who have said maybe, send an email suggesting a meeting time and place for you to talk further about what you're looking for.

d. Hold any scheduled meetings with potential volunteers.

e. For those who have said no,

- Move their names to the bottom of the pool list, under the section called "No."

- Beside each name, write what role each person has said no to.

- Remove their names from the needs list.

- Place new names in the blanks left by those who have said no.

f. Send your standard invitation email to the people you have added to your master recruiting list.

g. Send a follow-up message to any potential volunteer who hasn't responded to your last message in three days or more.

4. Take one more step for each of the five leader documents, either working on the document yourself or providing support to the person responsible to complete the document in the next two days:

   ○ youth leader directory

   ○ major event calendar

   ○ youth directory

   ○ child protection and screening forms and policies

   ○ job descriptions

Send a reminder to those working on these documents that you'll need a draft of what they have done by the end of the day tomorrow.

5. Take a look at the structure document you developed on day nineteen. Using the ranked list of your current volunteers, determine if anyone is in the "wrong seat on the bus." Make one step today toward moving someone on your current team into a role that will be more life-giving for the volunteer and more impactful for your ministry.

 **DAY 27**

Preparing for the Mess

> *Life isn't like a book.*
> *Life isn't logical or sensible or orderly.*
> *Life is a mess most of the time.*
>
> CHARLES CALEB COLTON

By now, there is a good chance you have your team in place. You may be breathing a well-deserved sigh of relief as you see the end in sight.

As you head into the new year with your new team, I want you to be prepared for what's coming. Something *will* go wrong. Despite your best efforts,

- There will be someone (or several someones) who thought they were agreeing to something very different than you did.

- There will be those who will do only *part* of the role they signed on for.

- Emergencies will come up that will require one or more of your leaders to bow out prematurely.

- Volunteers will get sideways with each other (or with you, with the leadership, with your church, with your denomination or with another person sitting in their pew).

There are two things you can do to prepare for the unexpected:

- Confirm expectations in writing with each of the volunteers who have said yes (which you have already done).

- Build in several one-on-one follow-up conversations in the first couple months for realignment and troubleshooting with your volunteers (which you will do today).

You'll seek to deal non-anxiously, non-reactively with each surprise as it comes. You'll go back to your master recruiting list when you need to; you'll re-edit job descriptions to meet the "twisted" needs of your team members; you'll find short-term solutions to work until you can arrive at permanent ones. When the unexpected does happen, you won't be surprised. In fact, you expected it.

Today's Mission

1. Thank God for the leaders who have agreed to serve with you in the coming year.

2. Complete the items you've assigned yourself to accomplish on this day. If you haven't scheduled specific items on this day, return to day twenty-three and complete step one.

3. Continue your recruiting and follow-up work:

    a. With your master recruiting documents (your needs list and your ranked pool list) in front of you, check your email to see if anyone has responded to your invitation and reply to those emails immediately.

    b. For those who have said yes, make sure their names are written in black ink on your master list.

c. For those who have said maybe, send an email suggesting a meeting time and place for you to talk further about what you're looking for.

d. Hold any scheduled meetings with potential volunteers.

e. For those who have said no,

- Move their names to the bottom of the pool list, under the section called "No."

- Beside each name, write what role each person has said no to.

- Remove their names from the needs list.

- Place new names in the blanks left by those who have said no.

f. Send your standard invitation email to the people you have added to your master recruiting list.

g. Send a follow-up message to any potential volunteer who hasn't responded to your last message in three days or more.

4. Continue working on the five leader documents and collect drafts of these documents from any people who are working on them for you:

- youth leader directory
- major event calendar
- youth directory
- child protection and screening forms and policies
- job descriptions

5. Take a look at the structure document from day nineteen. Using the ranked list of your current volunteers, determine if anyone is in the "wrong seat on the bus." Make one step today toward moving someone on your current team into a role that

will be more life-giving for the volunteer and more impactful for your ministry.

6. Build into your calendar the times you will be checking in personally with each of your volunteers over their first month for realignment and troubleshooting.

 **DAY 28**

Telling a Better Story

Whoever tells the best story wins.

ANNETTE SIMMONS

It has long been understood by culture watchers that the people who tell the best stories control the future.

Too many folks, when they are recruiting, simply tell lousy stories. Consider some of the worst we have heard (maybe you have heard them too):

- "We all know that high school kids just don't show up on Sunday mornings, but for the kids with no social life, we figured we'd need to have Sunday school. Would you be willing to teach?"

- "Youth group has never worked in our church, but our elders are demanding that we have a program 'for kids not to come to.' We're looking for someone to lead this group."

- "With all the trouble we've had in the church recently, none of the volunteers we've had working with our youth in the last ten years are around anymore. Some have moved to other churches; most have stopped going to church altogether."

- "We've never had anyone who could handle our youth group for more than six months. Would you be willing to give it a try?"

Whether it's with our volunteer teams or in any other area of your ministry, we've got to tell better stories. The stories we tell (and the ways we tell them) set the trajectory for the future of our ministries. In place of the lousy stories above, how about starting with these?

- "We've got a really committed, really unique group, just a few kids, who come on Sunday mornings. They are all so different, but they love to be together and they love being here. Would you consider joining the team working with them this next year?"

- "This is a rebuilding year for our youth ministry. Our church, particularly our elders, are behind it like I've never seen before. There are going to be a lot of bumps in the road and plenty of mess as we rebuild. But I can't think of anyone I'd rather have on the renovation team than you."

- "It's no secret that it's been a tough year for our church. One of the unexpected casualties of all that's been going on, though, has been our kids. We've got to turn our attention toward what they need now. I'm pulling together a team who will help bring healing to the most vulnerable group in our church. And I would love for you to be a part of it."

- "Our youth are desperately in need of consistency. They are a bit like foster children who have been passed from leader to leader for the past five years. I'm pulling together a team of three couples whose number-one job will be to be there for our kids for the next few years."

Each time we ask a volunteer to serve, we are telling a story that foreshadows for the potential leader either success or failure. As you ask, remember that "winning" always comes to those who tell the best stories.

Today's Mission

1. Complete the items you've assigned yourself to accomplish on this day. If you haven't scheduled specific items on this day, return to day twenty-three and complete step one.

2. Continue your recruiting and follow-up work:

    a. With your master recruiting documents (your needs list and your ranked pool list) in front of you, check your email to see if anyone has responded to your invitation and reply to those emails immediately.

    b. For those who have said yes, make sure their names are written in black ink on your master list.

    c. For those who have said maybe, send an email suggesting a meeting time and place for you to talk further about what you're looking for.

    d. Hold any scheduled meetings with potential volunteers.

    e. For those who have said no,

    - Move their names to the bottom of the pool list, under the section called "No."

    - Beside each name, write what role each person has said no to.

    - Remove their names from the needs list.

    - Place new names in the blanks left by those who have said no.

    f. Send your standard invitation email to the people you have added to your master recruiting list.

    g. Send a follow-up message to any potential volunteer who hasn't responded to your last message in three days or more.

3. Put the finishing touches on your key leader documents now that you've collected drafts from anyone who has agreed to help you with them.

   ○ youth leader directory

   ○ major event calendar

   ○ youth directory

   ○ child protection and screening forms and policies

   ○ job descriptions

4. Take a look at the structure document from day nineteen. Using the ranked list of your current volunteers, determine if anyone is in the "wrong seat on the bus." Make one step today toward moving someone on your current team into a role that will be more life-giving for the volunteer and more impactful for your ministry.

 **DAY 29**

Reflection Day

It's the Little Things

His master replied, "Well done, good and faithful servant!
You have been faithful with a few things;
I will put you in charge of many things."

MATTHEW 25:23

Over the past twenty-eight days, you have tried to be faithful in the little things. Whether it's investing our first moments each day in the presence of God, investing our first dollars instead of spending them or clothing our first words with our beloved each day in kindness, the road to transformation always comes on the path of the little things. It's the little, inconvenient kindnesses that keep a marriage alive, and it's the little daily decisions we make that transform our ministries from what they are to what we dream they can be.

One of the amazing things about the story of the sheep and the goats is that *both* groups were totally shocked. The simple acts of kindness they had (or had not) done were hardly memorable. Neither noticed the hidden presence of God in the little things they did (or didn't do) for the poor.

For the sheep—those who tended to the desperate needs around them—the list of accomplishments, frankly, doesn't make a very impressive résumé:

- "I was hungry and you gave me something to eat."
- "I was thirsty and you gave me something to drink."
- "I was a stranger and you invited me in."
- "I needed clothes and you clothed me."
- "I was sick and you looked after me."
- "I was in prison and you came to visit me." (Matthew 25:35-36)

But it is these fully forgettable acts that set the ultimate destiny of those who do them. We hope that in these last twenty-eight days, you have experienced the miraculous, transforming power of the little things.

Today is your final reflection day. You will have one more wrap-up meeting with your prayer partners within the next week. Today, you reflect and give thanks (or just take a break and think through the questions below when you meet with your prayer partners).

TODAY'S MISSION

1. Give thanks for all the leaders who have agreed to serve in your ministry in the coming year.

2. Send a text to your prayer partners, reminding them about your upcoming meeting and saying thanks for joining you in this process.

3. When you meet with your prayer partners, share your answers to these questions:

- What are you most excited about after having worked this
  process for a month?

- What have you learned about yourself and your ministry
  through this process?

- What might have made this process more effective or
  meaningful?

4. Invite your prayer partners to share their own responses to the
   three questions above.

5. Do a little "show and tell" with your prayer partners, showing
   your (hopefully completed) master recruiting list, as well as
   your volunteer recruitment and development manual.

 **DAY 30**

Final Balcony Day

*If we're going to grow up in Christ, we've got to change every day.
If we don't, we're not growing up in Christ . . .
we're just growing old in Christ.*

STEVE FARRAR

You know what you call someone who runs a marathon very slowly? A finisher.

The runner who finishes the 26.2 miles in 6 hours and 18 minutes gets the very same medal at the end of the race as the runner who finishes in 2 hours and 18 minutes.

Today you are finishing your thirty-day marathon. And you've likely learned a few things:

- You've learned that focus works, while random attention to a random collection of priorities seldom creates any real change.

- You've learned that with the structure you've put in place, building next year's volunteer team will not be nearly so time consuming.

- You've learned that, no matter how old you are or how much you have known about youth ministry, you have continued growing in your craft of ministry and in your love for God.

I hope you're feeling a little end-of-the-marathon, exhausted encouragement right about now. As you finish this project, pray one more time for each of the folks who will partner with you in ministry in the coming year. Thank God that you have been blessed with a team who will walk with you through (and periodically create some of!) the mess of ministry. And rest in the reality that you have invested in something that will bear more fruit year after year.

Congratulations, finisher.

Today's Mission

1. Compile all your volunteer documents into a single notebook or folder (either in a physical notebook or on the computer, with the file backed up and shared with at least two other people). You'll want to include your

   ○ youth leader directory

   ○ major event calendar

   ○ youth directory

   ○ child protection and screening forms and policies

   ○ job descriptions

   ○ letters or emails you have sent out that can be templates for the recruiting process next year

   ○ "Improving Our Recruiting Process" document, with notes you have kept throughout this process of things you'd like to do differently in recruiting next year

2. Select a date to begin the recruiting process next year, and mark it boldly on next year's calendars (your personal calendar and the ministry's major event calendar).

3. Send confirmation letters or emails, expressing your enthusiasm and gratitude to all the volunteers who have agreed to serve in the coming year, both partners and helpers (see sample below). Include

   ○ the individual's job description

   ○ their starting date for working with the youth

   ○ the date for the leader orientation

4. Double check to make sure that you have all your communication deadlines firmly on your calendar, including

   ○ when you will publically commission your leaders

   ○ when articles about your leadership team will appear in the church newsletter, on the church website, in the youth ministry newsletter, on your Facebook page and so on.

Note that in appendix four we've included a master task list outlining all the missions from day one to day thirty.

Sample volunteer confirmation email

> Dear [NAME],
>
> Thank you so much for your willingness to serve in our youth ministry this coming year! Your work as a [ROLE] will be invaluable for our church and our kids!
>
> The purpose of this email is to confirm the role that we have talked about for you and to give you a few details that will help you launch well.
>
> First, I have attached a copy of the job description we created for your role. Hopefully, what you find there matches what we have talked about. But if you see anything there that doesn't accurately reflect your under-

standing of what you agreed to, just let me know and we'll work through the concerns you have.

Second, I want to remind you about our youth ministry leadership team orientation dinner scheduled for [DATE AND TIME] at [PLACE, ADDRESS]. At this meeting, we'll be gathering all our key youth leaders for the fall. We'll be able to get through our business quickly and have plenty of time to enjoy getting to know each other afterward.

Third, your first day in your new role will be on [DAY, DATE] at [TIME] in [PLACE]. If you can arrive about fifteen minutes early, we'll have time to pray together with the other leaders and make sure all our bases are covered.

I'm so looking forward to working with you this year. Thanks again for saying yes!

Please call [NUMBER] or email [EMAIL] if you have any questions or things you need to let us know about.

Blessings,

[NAME]
[TITLE]

MINISTRY ARCHITECTS GUARANTEE

If you work this thirty-day process one to two hours a day, six days a week for thirty days and it does not create significant change in your ministry, Ministry Architects will gladly refund the cost of this book and offer a credit of $20 toward any downloadable resource in our online store at ministryarchitects.com. For both the refund and credit email info@marchitects.com

 **APPENDIX 1**

Eight Sample Messages for Recruiting

Message one: Hi Jill. It's Mark from church. I'm putting my team together to work with our seventh graders for next year, and I would love for you to think about being part of that group. Feel free to call me back with a "no" or a "maybe." If it's a maybe, let's get together and talk about it. If it's a no, I'll just call you in six months or a year to see if you might have seen a burning bush. My cell number is 555-5555 and my email address is Mark@yaya.com. Hope to hear from you soon.

Message two: Jill, it's Mark from church. Hope all is well in your world. I'm just circling around to see what you're thinking about the possibility of working with our seventh graders starting in the fall. You would be terrific! Feel free to call (555-5555) or email (Mark@yaya.com) any time. Have a great rest of the day!

Message three: Hey Jill, let me tell you why I'm excited! I'm excited because you haven't given me a "no" yet about working with our seventh graders. I'm thrilled you're still thinking about it! Give me a call whenever it's convenient for you (555-5555).

Message four: Hi Jill, it's your old friend Mark from church! You'll be thrilled to know that _____ has agreed to work with our new seventh graders starting in the fall. I think you guys would work beautifully together. You can just call me back with a "no" or a "maybe." If it's a maybe, I'd love to buy you some coffee and talk further. If it's a no, I'll ask about something else another time! My email is Mark@yaya.com.

Message five: Jill, my friend! I know your life is crazy right now, but I'm encouraged that I haven't heard a "no" from you yet! Our team really feels that you have the kind of gifts and personality and faith that we'd love for our seventh graders to be around. I look forward to hearing from you soon at 555-5555 or Mark@yaya.com. If I don't hear back from you in a couple days, I'll just call back.

Message six: Jill, are you feeling the love? It's Mark. Hopefully, you've heard in my previous messages how excited we'd be to have you on our team with our new seventh graders. I'm sure you've got a few questions. Just give me a call or an email, and you can give me a little clarity about what you're thinking: 555-5555 or Mark@yaya.com.

Message seven: Hi Jill! It's Mark. I'm here with our youth group right now. And they've got something to say to you [insert ca-cophony of kids yelling things like "You'll be great!" "Thanks for thinking about us!" "We want you!" all at the same time]. Great to be wanted, isn't it? Hope to hear from you soon. You've got my contact info, or you can just leave a message at the church on my voicemail at 222-2222.

Message eight: Okay, Jill. I'm not beyond bribery. How about you let me buy you lunch and we talk about this whole seventh grade leader thing. Let me know a good time for you. Mark@yaya .com. Have a great day!

 APPENDIX 2

Sample Major Event Calendar

Weekly Sunday Schedule: 6th–12th Grade

9:15 a.m.	Worship
10:20 a.m.	Refreshments and fellowship in gym
10:45–11:10 a.m.	Sunday school
	Locations:

	6th and 7th grades	200-202
	8th grade	203
	9th–12th grades	204-205
4:30–6:00 p.m.	Youth group in gym	

Youth Ministry Calendar

September 17	2014 youth ministry kick-off	
September 23	mission trip reunion dinner	6:00 p.m.
September 24	serve breakfast at Christian Service Center	6:45–8:15 a.m.
September 29	9th grade lock-in	7:00 p.m.–9:30 a.m.
September 30	8th grade confirmation meeting	9:00 a.m.–1:00 p.m.
October 1	Cardinals baseball game	1:15 p.m.
October 4	YM leadership team meeting	12:00–1:30 p.m.
October 14	all–youth group soccer game	3:00–5:00 p.m.
	MS hayride	Saturday night
October 22	serve breakfast at Christian Service Center	6:45–8:15 a.m.
October 23	evening prayer—all youth and families	5:30 p.m.
October 29	MS video scavenger hunt	4:00–6:00 p.m.
November 1	Sunday school teacher training and lunch	12:00 p.m.
November 1	parenting seminar	7:00 p.m.
November 3	YM leadership team meeting	12 noon
November 4	Blockbuster service event	1:00–4:00 p.m.
November 8	healing service—youth and families	5:30 p.m.
November 26	serve breakfast at Christian Service Center	6:45–8:15 a.m.
December 3	Journey to Bethlehem	4:30–8:00 p.m.
December 6	Student Great Wednesdays	6:00–8:00 p.m.
December 10	St. Nicholas breakfast	9:00 a.m.–12:00 p.m.
December 13	Student Great Wednesdays	6:00–8:00 p.m.

Date	Event	Time
December 17	YM Christmas caroling	5:00–7:00 p.m.
December 20	2006 HS graduate reunion	12:00–1:30 p.m.
	Student Great Wednesdays	6:00–8:00 p.m.
December 24	serve breakfast at Christian Service Center	6:45–8:15 a.m.
	8th grade Gospel Pageant	4:00 p.m.
January 3	YM leadership team meeting	
January 6–7	HS retreat	
January 15	paint the youth room day	
January 20–21	MS retreat	
January 28	serve breakfast at Christian Service Center	6:45–8:15 a.m.
January 31	YM family night—Bible Jeopardy	6:00–8:00 p.m.
February 3	8th grade confirmation meeting	9:00 a.m.–3:00 p.m.
February 7	YM leadership team meeting	
February 10	skiing at Hidden Valley	8:00 a.m.–4:00 p.m.
February 20	pancake supper	5:30–7:00 p.m.
February 21	Ash Wednesday service	
February 25	serve breakfast at Christian Service Center	6:45–8:15 a.m.
	Sunday school teacher lunch	11:15 a.m.–12:15 p.m.
February 28	Student Great Wednesdays	6:00–8:00 p.m.
March 3	Blockbuster service event	1:00–4:00 p.m.
March 7	Student Great Wednesdays	6:00–8:00 p.m.
March 14	Student Great Wednesdays	6:00–8:00 p.m.
March 21	Student Great Wednesdays	6:00–8:00 p.m.
March 25	serve breakfast at Christian Service Center	6:45–8:15 a.m.
April 1	Palm Sunday	
April 4	YM leadership team meeting	
April 5	Maundy Thursday	
April 6	Good Friday	
April 7	Easter Vigil	
April 8	Easter	
April 15	HS youth group	4:30–6:00 p.m.
April 22	serve breakfast at Christian Service Center	6:45–8:15 a.m.
April 29	8th grade breakfast celebration	8:00–9:00 a.m.
May 6	5th grade welcome into YM	10:30–11:15 a.m.
May 7	SS teacher/YM leadership team appreciation dinner	
May 11	confirmation evening prayer/dinner	6:00–8:00 p.m.
May 12	Confirmation Sunday	11:00 a.m.
May 13	recognition of confirmands and reception	

May 22	serve breakfast at Christian Service Center	6:45–8:15 a.m.
June 3	HS graduate commissioning and reception	10:00 a.m.
June 10	youth ministry Family Float Trip	
June 25	serve breakfast at Christian Service Center	6:45–8:15 a.m.
July 8–14	2015 youth mission trip	
July 23	serve breakfast at Christian Service Center	6:45–8:15 a.m.
August 19	mission trip slide show (between services)	
August 26	6th grade rite of passage	

 **APPENDIX 3**

Sample Helper Role Survey

[Church Name]
Youth Ministry Helper Survey
[Year]

Name: _____

Preferred phone: _____

Email: _____

Spouse: _____

Preferred phone: _____

Email: _____

Name and grade of students in 7th–12th grade:

_____

_____

_____

One of the dreams of our youth ministry is that every youth parent serve in at least one youth ministry program each year. Please review the list below and check any roles that sound like a fit for you. Thanks so much for your support.

___ Help with a grade-level event

___ Help with a grade-level service project

___ Serve as a basketball coach

___ Serve as a prayer partner for a youth

___ Help with Crud Day (September of each year)

___ I want to be a coach   ___ I want to be a safety spotter

___ I'll do anything;   ___ I want a clean job

Volunteer Teams

Each year, countless volunteers are needed to develop and present each of our major events. By joining a team, you are not required to work every event but are asked to help on your team whenever you are able.

____ **Team Invitations:** Work with event chairs to design and create invitations for major events or simply help with printing, stuffing, addressing, sealing, stamping and mailing.

____ **Team Decorations:** Work with event chairs to design, create and implement themes and decorations for the Prayer Partner Banquet, Fall Kick-off, Crud Day and Family Face Lift.

____ **Team Food:** Work with event chairs to plan, procure and serve food for major events.

____ **Team Tech:** Work with event chairs to determine audio/visual needs for slide shows, lighting, sound, recorded music and possibly bands.

____ **Team Muscles:** Work with event chairs to break down and neatly stack chairs and tables and help with cleanup after major events.

____ **Team Photography:** Work with event chairs to ensure photos are taken at all events. Also work with youth staff once in the fall and once in the spring to organize photos into students' files (staff will identify students).

Please return this survey via email to suzie@yaya.com or mail it to Suzie Coordinator at 55552 North Church Street, Youth City, NY 33333.

 **APPENDIX 4**

Master Summary Task List

1. Scan through the entire thirty-day plan (this book) to get a sense of the rhythms of the weeks.

2. Answer this question in writing, and be prepared to share your response with your prayer partners when you meet with them: *At the end of this 30-Day Change, how would you like your ministry to be different?* (Hints: How many volunteers? What kinds of volunteers? What's different about the recruiting process? The training process? How does it feel different?). You might know you've got this right when you read it and it creates a little lump in your throat.

3. Invite two people to be your prayer partners through this thirty-day process—to pray for you and for the process, and to meet with you weekly to help you think through the implementation steps found in the next twenty-nine days. Suggest meeting times, ideally in a rhythm that lines up with your reflection days (days 8, 15, 22, 29).

4. Send an email or text or make a call to at least three previous volunteers who have left the youth ministry (or maybe even the church) in the last year or two. Let them know a little about this project, and invite them to give you feedback to help you understand each of their particular reasons for no longer working as a volunteer. (See day 1 for a sample email you could send, including a few key questions to ask.)

5. Determine what day you will carve out as your reflection day (or sabbath day) each week. On reflection days, the assignments will

take much less time. We have provided questions for you to work through in preparation for your weekly check-in with your prayer partners. Once you have determined when your reflection day will be each week, orient your thirty-day project around those days. For example, if you determine your reflection days will be on Thursdays, select a Thursday at least eight days away and make that day eight of this project. Make the day before day seven, and the day after day nine. Keep numbering days accordingly until all thirty have been assigned to a specific day on the calendar.

6. For each of the non-reflection days, schedule two hours a day to focus on your 30-Day Change project. It may not take two hours every day, but having the time set aside will ensure that you have appropriate margin to accomplish each 30-Day Change daily mission.

7. Begin to compile your 30-Day Change resource pile (or notebook, if you happen to experience pile aversion). By the end of your first week you will have added a number of items to this pile, but on this day include

   o your church directory, ideally a pictorial one but definitely one with easily accessible contact information, including email addresses

   o a list of current volunteer leaders with their contact information

   o a list of all previous leaders from the past five to ten years, if possible

   o this book if you've got it in printed form

8. Create a photo wall of all your current leaders, to be used when you meet with your prayer partners to pray for each of those leaders by name. Each time a new leader is added to your team, include his or her picture on the prayer wall.

9. Take a quick inventory of your current leaders by answering these questions:

   o Which of my current leaders is exactly in the right role—not overwhelmed or under-challenged?

   o Is there anyone on the team who would be delighted to do more if asked?

   o Is there anyone on the team desperately in need of a break?

   o Which leader is in the "wrong seat on the bus"?

10. Lock in your meeting times with your prayer partners for the next month.

11. Create a list of the top five challenges to having the kind of volunteer team you want in your ministry.

12. Develop your needs list for partner volunteers. You can use the downloadable 30-Day Change Master Needs Template or make your own list on paper based on what you see there. Include all the partner roles you will need for the coming year in your ministry.

13. Once you have completed the list of all your needed partner volunteers, count how many slots there are on your list. We're looking here for the total number of people you will need, not the number of different roles. So if you need six Sunday school teachers in one setting, that counts as six, not one.

14. Multiply by three the number of needed partner volunteers (determined in step 13 above). For example, if you need twenty-five partner volunteers, multiply twenty-five by three and get seventy-five. (We're really not trying to make this feel like your 1040 tax form!)

15. Follow up with any of the three previous volunteers (step 4) you haven't heard from to gather their input as you begin this project.

16. Review the partner needs list you developed. See if there are any positions you need to add or if you want to change the number of leaders needed for any given category, and update the list accordingly.

17. Create a potential volunteer pool list with the same number of blanks as the number you ended up with in step fourteen. Come up with names of everyone you can think of in your church who might be a potential volunteer. At this point you are not filtering or excluding any names, just including anyone you think might have potential, whether you think they will say yes or not. Here are a couple of places to look for your potential volunteers:

    o Look through your church's directory to be prompted about people who might serve as volunteers.

    o Since it's likely that you don't know everyone in your church, reach out to ten or so folks who can serve as sources for you (see day 4 for a sample email). You'll want to keep asking until you come up with as many names as your target potential volunteer number. Send an email to

    • your colleagues on staff

    • well-networked parents

    • student leaders

    • current volunteer leaders

    • church leadership—elders, deacons, adult Sunday school teachers

    • saints and pillars of your church

18. Create a document called "Improving Our Recruiting Process" (either on your computer or in a physical file). As you come across things you'd like to do differently when you start the recruiting process a year from now, include those ideas in this document.

19. On your potential pool list, write to the left side of each name one of the following letters:

   A—This person would be a *great* addition to your team.

   B—This person would be a good addition to your team.

   C—This person is a possible addition to your team.

20. To the right side of the names on your list, identify each person with one of the following letters:

   W—This person would be great working *with* kids.

   B—This person would be great working *behind* the scenes.

   E—This person would be great working in *either* kind of role—with kids or behind the scenes.

21. Place names from your pool list into your master needs list so that every blank has a single name in it. Each name should only be used once. You'll want to place the A names first, placing Ws and Es in roles working directly with students and Bs and Es in behind-the-scenes roles. You can see a sample master needs list at ministryarchitects.com/30-day-change-resources.

22. On your master needs list, include a phone number and email address for every name you have placed in a slot.

23. Now that you've matched your pool list with your needs list and every blank is filled, it's time to get a single ask out to every person on your master needs list (which we'll also call the master recruiting list now that names are added) by sending a personal email (like the one on the next page) to each one.

Hey [NAME],

I hope all is well in your world.

I've got a quick question for you, one that I realize may not have a quick answer!

I'm putting together my team for next year's _____ [for example, seventh grade Sunday school, small group program], and I would love for you [or you and spouse— using his or her name] to consider being a part of this team.

You may know right now that you can't take on another thing next year, starting [DATE]. If so, just give me a quick "call me another year" message, and I'll get back to you in six months or so. If you're a "maybe," let me know and I can give you a little more detail about what we're looking for and give you the chance to ask any questions you might have.

There are a handful of folks in the church who get to work with our teenagers, and I'd love for you to be one of them next year!

I look forward to hearing from you.

24. Take out your master recruiting documents: your needs list and your ranked pool list. Check your email to see if anyone has responded to your email invitation and reply to those emails immediately. For those who have said yes, send an email suggesting a meeting time and place for you to talk further about what you're looking for. For those who have said no,

   o Move their names to the bottom of the pool list, under a new section called "No."

- Beside each name, write what role each person has said no to.

- Remove their names from the needs list.

- Place new names in the blanks left by those who have said no.

25. Send your standard invitation email to the people you have added to your master recruiting list.

26. Each time you meet with your prayer partners, pray over the names of potential volunteers, share your updated master recruiting documents and share your answers to these questions:

    - What are you most excited about after having worked this process so far?

    - What has been your biggest point of discouragement?

    - As you look at the next week, what times have you set aside to focus on the assignments you've been given?

    - How can your prayer partners be praying for you this week, whether about this 30-Day Change process or about anything else that you're experiencing as particularly pressing at this point in your life?

27. Make a master list of all those who have said yes to specific roles. Print out the list of names and roles and display it prominently in your office.

28. Each week of these thirty days, take a look at your task list for the week (or create one if this is not a natural part of the rhythm of your life yet). Identify your top priorities for the week. You are looking here for things that will make your life and ministry more how you'd like them to be a year from now (not the screaming, urgent demands on your time). Your top priorities might include

- deliberate time with your family,

- time for specific spiritual disciplines

- and (of course) during these thirty days, two hours daily focused on building your volunteer team.

29. Each week of these thirty days, complete your calendar for the week, including all currently scheduled appointments (meetings, programs and any other commitments). Now make appointments with yourself for your top priorities you identified in step twenty-eight.

30. You may very well find that when you add your currently scheduled commitments and top priorities, you are already out of time for the week (and you still have a few urgent things you've got to get to, not to mention returning emails and messages). On some weeks this is *normal*. If this is the case for you this week, you've got some problem solving to do. Here's a start:

- Corral your emails and phone calls into a specific time block for each day. If your week is packed, you simply don't have time to be immediately available this week. Plan on taking a break from Facebook and Twitter as well.

- Determine what will need to be cut from your schedule, being careful not to cut any of your top priorities (those things that have the potential to make your life and ministry different a year from now). You may need to reschedule a meeting or two, delegate or simply live with the possibility that there may be some part of your life that is less excellent this week. If this feels foreign to you, remember that this is something you actually do every week already. It's just that you do it on the fly, later in the week, and (if you're like most of us) you wind up sacrificing your most important priorities.

○ Keep working on the filtering process until you have a schedule for the week that allows time for your most important priorities, time for current appointments and a few hours of margin.

31. Determine all the job descriptions you need for your ministry by making a list of all the positions, volunteer and paid, that it takes to run your ministry effectively. Be sure to include paid staff and helpers (drivers, meal providers, etc.) as well as partners (small group leaders, Sunday school teachers, major event coordinators, etc.). Remember, at this point you're not only listing the positions you currently have but all those you hope to have in the coming year.

32. Identify the job descriptions that are your highest priority— likely the partner roles that you are spending time recruiting for right now.

33. Draft job descriptions for all your partner roles as well as for any paid staff in your ministry. (Go to ministryarchitects.com/30-day -change-resources for samples you can edit.) Make sure you include how long the commitment is as well as the schedule of when meetings for coordination, planning and training will take place.

34. Meet face-to-face with any potential volunteers who have agreed to a meeting.

   a. Bring the job description for the specific role for which you would like this person's help.

   b. Begin the conversation by listening to your potential recruit to learn what they are thinking and feeling about the opportunity and to learn any concerns they might have.

   c. Address their concerns with joyful clarity, being sure to ask for what you really need. It may be that at this point you discover that you have someone willing to *help* but not willing to be a partner. If this is the case, do not slot this person into a partner role. Go back and find another person who might serve in the partner role, and celebrate that this person will be a helper.

35. Get into a rhythm of doing follow-up recruiting work daily:

   a. Take out your master recruiting documents: your needs list and your ranked pool list.

   b. Check your email to see if anyone has responded to your email invitation, and reply to those emails immediately.

   c. For those who have said yes, send an email suggesting a meeting time and place for you to talk further about what you're looking for.

   d. For those who have said no,

   - Move their names to the bottom of the pool list under the section called "No."

   - Beside each name, write what role each person has said no to.

   - Remove their names from the needs list.

   e. Place new names in the blanks left by those who have said no.

   f. Send your standard invitation email to the people you have added to your master recruiting list.

   g. Follow up with those who have not responded to your last message in three days or more.

36. Rework your sourcing process:

   a. Contact five people in your church whom you may not know very well, let them know that you are in the process of building your youth ministry team for the coming year and ask them if they have noticed anyone in the church who they think might have gifts for working with youth.

b. Contact five parents of some of your more enthusiastically involved youth and ask them for the names of anyone they would recommend as a potential leader.

c. Ask your colleagues on staff again for the names of any people they may not have thought of a couple weeks ago.

d. Scan through the church directory to see if there might be someone there you've missed.

e. Remember to look around on Sunday morning and see if there might be someone you want to ask others in the congregation about.

f. Add any new names to your master recruiting list and rank them (ABC, WEB) as you have the others.

37. Refresh your master recruiting list:

a. Add to your master recruiting list any additional names of new potential volunteers that might have bubbled up in your sourcing process.

b. Make sure everyone on your pool list is appropriately categorized:

- Those who have said no are taken out of the master list and put at the bottom of the list, each with a note indicating what roles they said no to.

- Those you're still waiting to hear back from are highlighted in some way, with indications for each of how many messages you have left.

- Those who have said yes are written into your master needs list in big, black marker.

38. Answer the following pre-calendaring questions:

    o How often do you want your leaders to be together, just as leaders, over the span of a year?

    o What would you like to do for an orientation for your leaders at the beginning of the year?

    o What would you like to do to celebrate the work the leaders have done at the end of the year?

    o What would you like to do to ensure that the leaders who can't (or won't) make the meetings have access to the training and to the sense of connection that will take place at the meetings?

    o Are there any other special times you'd like your team to be together—maybe a Christmas party, a commissioning service or a community training you'd like to promote?

    At this point, don't worry too much about what's realistic. Start with what you'd love to see happen in terms of the rhythm of your leader gatherings.

39. Pull out your master ministry calendar for the coming year (if you don't have one yet, this would be a good time to create the first draft). Most youth pastors choose to schedule their leader events from August or September of the coming year through July or August of the next year. Ideally, you want to start with a calendar that (1) enables you to look at the entire year at one time and (2) includes key programming and holidays for the entire year.

40. With a *pencil*, calendar leader gatherings for the coming year, prompted by the five pre-calendaring questions.

41. Once you've got all the dates on the calendar based on your responses to the pre-calendaring questions, look at the flow of the ministry year and make adjustments as needed. For example, on closer examination you may discover that you've

planned a leader dinner for Super Bowl Sunday or that you've planned your big leader orientation meeting on a Saturday morning that conflicts with a school fundraiser in your town. Make adjustments as needed.

42. Check in with two or three of your current key volunteers, email them a copy of your calendar and gather their feedback on your leader-development calendar for the coming year. Make adjustments to the calendar based on their feedback.

43. Pull out the list of all your current leaders and rank each one's satisfaction level, as you imagine it, regarding their role in the ministry:

    o **A rank of 1** means that they are doing work that makes their heart sing, and they come away from their work in your ministry almost always grateful and delighted to have served.

    o **A rank of 2** means that they feel their work is making a difference and they are committed to it, even if at times it feels like an obligation.

    o **A rank of 3** means that they are willing to keep their commitment for this year but will probably quit at the end of the year. They have determined that the payoff is not worth their investment.

    o **A rank of 4** means that they are unhappy in their roles and are likely to drop out soon if changes aren't made.

    o **A rank of 5** means that you have no idea how satisfied they are in their roles.

44. For those with a rank of 5, call or send an email and have them rank themselves according to one of the first four categories.

45. Draft an organizational chart for your ministry. Make sure that it is easily editable and that it clearly shows who is responsible

for what *and* who is responsible if that person doesn't get his or her job done. Remember, this is not so much a program description chart as it is a responsibility chart. Go to ministry architects.com/30-day-change-resources to download sample youth ministry organizational charts.

46. Take a look at the structure document you developed on day nineteen or in step forty-five above. Using the ranked list of your current volunteers, determine if anyone is in the "wrong seat on the bus." Move everyone on your current team into a role that will be more life-giving for the volunteer and more impactful for your ministry.

47. Take stock of any loose ends from the past twenty-two days.

    o Review the daily assignments from past days.

    o Create a written list of all the items that remain incomplete. (If you are reading this book electronically, you can create the list through the highlighting feature on your reader.)

    o For each item on the "remaining items" list, estimate how much time the task will take.

    o Knowing that you really have six days left to complete these outstanding tasks, schedule time to complete each of them during the coming week. Once you have determined how much time each task will require, add 20 percent to that number of minutes and schedule those times in your calendar.

    o Repeat this process for these newly found items as part of Today's Mission on days twenty-four through thirty.

48. Develop your potential helper list, drawing on the names of those who have said no to a specific partner role but who you think might be willing to serve in a one-time helper role sometime during the year.

49. Edit the helper role survey, which includes a sample list of helper roles, to personalize it for your church. It is available in appendix three or at ministryarchitects.com/30-day-change-resources.

50. Send an email with the helper survey you edited to all your potential helpers.

51. Develop a calendar for how you will spread the viral good news about the strong youth ministry volunteer team in place for the coming year. Consider the following:

    ○ Include a celebration of the new volunteer team in the church newsletter.

    ○ Report the names and roles of your new volunteer team to the church's leadership.

    ○ Have a special program for the youth (and their parents) at which the new volunteers are celebrated and introduced.

    ○ Commission the volunteer team before the congregation.

    ○ Write an article for your church's website about the new team of volunteers.

    ○ Introduce and celebrate your new team of volunteers on the youth ministry's Facebook page.

52. Thank God for the leaders who have agreed to serve with you in the coming year.

53. Build into your calendar times you will be checking in personally with each of your volunteers over their first month for realignment and troubleshooting.

54. When you meet with your prayer partners, share your answers to these questions and invite them to share their responses as well:

    ○ What are you most excited about after having worked this process for a month?

- What have you learned about yourself and your ministry through this process?

- What might have made this process more effective or meaningful?

Do a little show and tell with your prayer partners, showing your (hopefully completed) master recruiting list, as well as your volunteer recruitment and development manual.

55. Compile all your volunteer documents into a single notebook or folder (either in a physical notebook or on the computer, with the file backed up and shared with at least two other people). You'll want to include your

   - youth leader directory

   - major event calendar

   - youth directory

   - child protection and screening forms and policies

   - job descriptions

   - letters or emails you have sent out that can be templates for the recruiting process next year

   - "Improving Our Recruiting Process" document, with notes you have kept throughout this process of things you'd like to do differently in recruiting next year

56. Select a date to begin the recruiting process next year and mark it boldly on next year's calendars (your personal calendar and the ministry's major event calendar).

57. Send a confirmation letter or email expressing your enthusiasm and gratitude to all the volunteers who have agreed to serve in the coming year, both partners and helpers. Include

   - the individual's job description

   o their starting date for working with the youth

   o the date of the leader orientation

58. Double-check to make sure that you have all your communication deadlines firmly on your calendar, including

   o when you will publically commission your leaders

   o when articles about your leadership team will appear in the church newsletter, on the church website, in the youth ministry newsletter, on your Facebook page and so on.

Notes

Introduction

[1]Peter Drucker, "On Managerial Courage," Harvard Business School Working Knowledge, June 12, 2006, htttp://hbswk.hbs.edu/archive/5377.html.

[2]A version of this article was originally published in *Group Magazine*, March-April 2009.

Day One

[1]Karen E. Jones and Dave Rahn, *Youth Ministry That Transforms: A Comprehensive Analysis of the Hopes, Frustrations, and Effectiveness of Today's Youth Workers* (Grand Rapids: Zondervan, 2001).

[2]This section is excerpted from Mark DeVries, *Sustainable Youth Ministry* (Downers Grove, IL: InterVarsity Press, 2008), pp. 145-47.

Day Nineteen

[1]Jim Collins, *Good to Great: Why Some Companies Make the Leap . . . and Others Don't* (New York: HarperCollins, 2001), p. 13.

Building Sustainable Ministries . . . One Church at a Time
www.ministryarchitects.com

Churches today face a tough reality: they desperately want to build thriving ministries, but the gap between aspiration and reality often feels insurmountable. Most simply resort to quick-fix solutions. These churches can easily become mired in a climate of criticism and complaint, as leaders and parents and pastors become increasingly obsessed with finding simple and immediate solutions.

But thriving, sustainable ministries are not built just because well-meaning leaders cobble together a disjointed collection of ideas from the most popular models, books and seminars. No, sustainable ministries take place when the church takes the time to "build the dance floor."

At Ministry Architects, we believe there is a better way—a better way than one-size-fits-all training events and quick-fix searches for superstar staffers. It all starts with building intentionally.

We have no interest in telling churches what they want to build. We start by listening and together develop a blueprint for moving from where they are to where they want to be. Then we walk alongside them to ensure that the renovation takes place in a sustainable way.

Ministry Architects partners with churches and their various ministries, working alongside key stakeholders to customize strategic plans for building successful and sustainable ministries.

For information about Ministry Architects or to schedule an assessment or other consulting services, visit ministryarchitects.com or contact us at info@ministryarchitects.com or 877-462-5718.

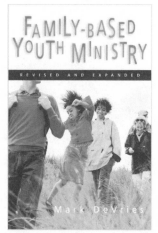

Family-Based Youth Ministry
978-0-8308-3243-9

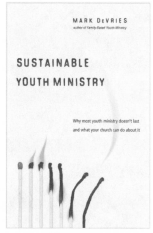

Sustainable Youth Ministry
978-0-8308-3361-0

IVP PRAXIS

EQUIPPING LEADERS FOR MINISTRY

God has called us to ministry. But it's not enough to have a vision for ministry if you don't have the practical skills for it. Nor is it enough to do the work of ministry if what you do is headed in the wrong direction. We need both vision *and* expertise for effective ministry. We need *praxis*.

Praxis puts theory into practice. It brings cutting-edge ministry expertise from visionary practitioners. You'll find sound biblical and theological foundations for ministry in the real world, with concrete examples for effective action and pastoral ministry. Praxis books are more than the "how to" – they're also the "why to." And because *being* is every bit as important as *doing*, Praxis attends to the inner life of the leader as well as the outer work of ministry. Feed your soul, and feed your ministry.

If you are called to ministry, you know you can't do it on your own. Let Praxis provide the companions you need to equip God's people for life in the kingdom.

www.ivpress.com/praxis